The Female Advantage

THE
Female Advantage

Women's Ways of Leadership

Sally Helgesen

DOUBLEDAY
CURRENCY

New York   London   Toronto   Sydney   Auckland

A CURRENCY PAPERBACK
PUBLISHED BY DOUBLEDAY
a division of Bantam Doubleday Dell Publishing Group, Inc.
1540 Broadway, New York, New York 10036

CURRENCY and DOUBLEDAY are trademarks of Doubleday,
a division of Bantam Doubleday Dell Publishing Group, Inc.

The Female Advantage was originally published in hardcover
by Currency Doubleday, a division of Bantam Doubleday Dell
Publishing Group, Inc., in 1990. The Currency Paperback edition
published by arrangement with Doubleday.

The excerpt on pages 265–72 is from *The Web of Inclusion*,
copyright © 1995 by Sally Helgesen.

Designed by Ann Gold

The Library of Congress has cataloged the Currency hardcover edition as follows:
Helgensen, Sally, 1948–
    The female advantage: women's ways of leadership /
by Sally Helgesen.
    p.   cm.
    1. Women executives—United States—Case studies.
2. Executive ability—Case studies.
3. Leadership—Case studies.   I. Title.
HD6054.4.U6H45   1990   89-48843
658.4'092'082—dc20   CIP

The Female Advantage is a federally registered trademark of Sally Helgesen.

ISBN 0-385-41911-2
Copyright © 1990 by Sally Helgesen
Introduction to the Paperback Edition and
User's Guide © 1995 by Sally Helgesen
All Rights Reserved
Printed in the United States of America
First Currency Paperback Edition: May 1995

10   9   8   7   6   5   4   3   2   1

FOR MY SISTERS, REBECCA, MARTHA, AND CECE,
AND MY SISTER-IN-LAW TONI.

Acknowledgments

Thanks for their help to four friends: Elizabeth Bailey, Marjory Bassett, Kathleen Cox and Stanley Crouch. Also and especially to my editor Harriet Rubin, for having the vision, seeing me through, and providing constant inspiration, encouragement, ideas and guidance. And to Nancy Evans for her faith, and for putting me together with Harriet.

C O N T E N T S

CONTENTS

Suppose Truth is a woman, what then?

—Nietzsche

INTRODUCTION TO THE
PAPERBACK EDITION

The Female Advantage made its way into the world in hardcover in May of 1990. Like many books that seem to find their readership at the precise right moment in time, this one reflected my personal experience in a way that mirrored the experience of others, although I could not have known that when the book was published. I had written it simply because working for a variety of companies over the years had convinced me that most organizations had absolutely no idea how to take advantage of the talents, skills, and ideas of the ever-increasing number of women who were joining their ranks.

By the late 1980s, we had entered upon a period of unprecedented organizational upheaval, which, if anything, has intensified during the past few years. Organizations of every variety—business, educational, governmental, legal, medical, religious—were being pressed to explore new styles of leadership, new structures, new ways of motivating people, new ways of strengthening relationships of every kind. At the same time that this was happening, women in substantial numbers were beginning to assume positions of real authority and influence within the public sphere. As historical outsiders to such positions, women often had fresh eyes to see what was no longer working and to identify new solutions. In addition, women were bringing into the workplace talents that had for years been considered of value only in the private, domestic sphere. Thus, women comprised a great resource for organizations seeking to adapt to dramatically altered circumstances. Their entrance into the public arena was occurring at just the right time.

Despite this fortunate confluence between what organizations needed and what women had to offer, most of the literature about women in the workplace still focused on their supposed handicaps: what skills they lacked, what they needed to learn, why they had to change. Women were taken to task for being insufficiently appreciative of the niceties of rank and distinction, for being too focused on the importance of relationships, for failing to appreciate business as some kind of giant game. A common bit of wisdom at the time held that because most women had not played football, they were poor at grasping the essentials of teamwork. As late as 1989, we were being urged to study diagrams of football plays in order to develop our capacity for strategic thinking.

In addition to cataloging these alleged handicaps, most popular literature was full of warnings that women should adapt to organizations *as they found them*. It was considered ruinous for women to draw attention to themselves—and thus to their presumed shortcomings—by trying to change how organizations were structured or run. We were told that we must adjust to the workplace rather than expect the workplace to adjust to us. In particular, we were urged to develop a greater appreciation for the workings of the hierarchy, and to downplay any reservations we might have about its effectiveness. After all, hierarchy had been the dominant mode of structuring institutions since Caesar organized the Roman army. Why should the entrance of women onto the public stage alter this?

I was convinced that the insistence that women should not expect to effect substantial change was bad both for women and for organizations. Precisely because most companies and institutions were facing radical and profound challenges, we had an enormous contribution to make. A negative focus at this particular time could thus prove especially unfortunate, since it might cause us to squander a historic opportunity to be agents of transformation.

It seemed clear that a positive look at what women had to offer was needed, so I undertook such a study. My intention was both to identify the characteristics that the best women leaders were bringing to their organizations and to examine the appropriateness of these characteristics for the kinds of demands organizations were facing. I began by interviewing scores of women, but was then persuaded by my editor, Harriet Rubin, to adopt instead a diary study approach. And so I stopped merely asking women how they led, or discussing philosophies of leadership, and began following leading women executives around during the course of their days. This approach enabled me more clearly to identify common characteristics, and also to make comparisons between the women I chose to study and a group of male executives that Henry Mintzberg had made the subject of diary studies some years before. Another invaluable result of using the diary method, although I didn't realize at the time, was that it would enable readers to use the women in the book as models in developing their own leadership styles. Because *The Female Advantage* concentrated on details rather than on grand overarching strategies or ideas, it came to serve women all over the country as a kind of training manual.

In retrospect, I realize that I had no idea how the book would be received when it came out. Its positive message was out of step with the conventional wisdom of the time. In addition, in 1990 it was still considered dangerous to discuss women in the workplace in terms of what specific skills or attitudes they might have to offer. Any examination of "difference" was considered akin to stereotyping—inevitably undermining women's ability to achieve high positions—rather than as a way of broadening the base of leadership styles recognized by the marketplace.

But the world has changed a lot over the last five years. The increasing recognition that the traditional hierarchy no longer mirrors how our technology works has made people eager to look at new ways of structuring organizations. And the steep decline of some of America's most successful companies has made many skeptical of traditional methods of command and control, and more willing to challenge received ideas about what constitutes effective leadership. But perhaps most important, women's growing experience in the workplace has made them more confident about asserting the value of what they have to bring to the public sphere. Inquiries into women's ways of working and communicating are no longer automatically viewed as threatening their progress but, rather, have become part of a larger discussion that has as its aim the development of more balanced and fully individuated leaders.

I believe that the unexpected and continuing success that *The Female Advantage* has enjoyed in the first half of this decade is the result of this changed environment. What I am really saying, I guess, is that it had timing on its side. This has been reflected in the way people have responded to the book. I remember the first letter I received, from a woman in Hutchinson, Kansas, who happened to be in a bookstore when it first arrived. Having just returned to work after many years at home with her children, she was feeling discouraged and out of place, unsure of the worth or appropriateness of her talents. Reading the book, and recognizing herself in the women leaders profiled, assured her that indeed she had something valuable to offer, something strong and unique. "What you describe in the book is very much how I do things. I thought it was just *my* style, but now I see that it's *a* style, and a good one!"

As I read that letter, I realized that *The Female Advantage* had found its market. Women like the one in Kansas were growing tired of being told that they didn't have the talents, toughness, experience, or image that they needed to be successful. As my volume of mail increased over the years, I also heard from men who saw themselves in the diary studies. Indeed, Ric Giardina of Intel, one of the heroes of my new book, *The Web of Inclusion*, first came to my attention when he wrote me to say that reading *The Female Advantage* had helped him understand why he had never been comfortable in organizations characterized by the traditional top-down style. As I make clear in *The Web of Inclusion*, the alternative style of leadership—which I first saw while studying women who came very much as outsiders to traditional organizations—is moving beyond gender in response to organizational need.

People often ask what surprised me most about the response to *The Female Advantage*. Most unexpected was the reaction from people in the military. I probably received as many letters from people in the U.S. armed services as from any other group, and the book was widely reviewed in service publications. General Perry Smith of the U.S. Army War College began a correspondence; the U.S. Air War College invited me to participate in a weeklong seminar. My contact with people of all ranks taught me that our services are ahead of many business organizations in terms of their commitment to changing the most profound essentials of how they are structured and run.

I remember one rainy evening in Reston, Virginia, when I spoke at a large nondenominational church that was sponsoring a series of lectures. Flying down, I had no idea how many military people lived in the area; that evening, the church's big lecture room was packed with Navy people. After my speech, I found myself engaged in one of the most stimulating and far-reaching discussions of my life, as people talked about how to transform an institution that has served as the very *pattern* of hierarchy in the Western world. That evening, I learned that the military not only is grappling with every major issue of culture change—the integration of women into field positions, the need to operate much more leanly, the demands of adapting a top-down system to a technology that empowers the ranks—but is having to do so in advance of most institutions.

Discussions such as I had that night, along with the letters I've received, have painted for me a vivid picture of an enormous transformation that is taking place all over the United States. Thousands of people are thinking in large and searching ways about how our organizations can best adapt to a radically changing world, and what those changes are going to mean for all of us. In particular, people are recognizing that the entrance of women—who represent one half of the human race—into public positions of authority for the first time in history must inevitably reconfigure every aspect of our common culture. We now have a chance to achieve a kind of balance in our institutions that has been painfully absent since the dawn of the Industrial Era. As I consider the transformations in consciousness (there is no other word) that are presently taking place, I find it nearly impossible not to be optimistic.

In the five years since the original publication of *The Female Advantage*, the lives of the women leaders whom I studied have changed. Frances Hesselbein retired from the Girls Scouts of the U.S.A. after fourteen years as National Executive Director. Although when she left the Girl Scouts she envisioned spending time at her Pennsylvania country house and writing a book, she very quickly accepted the position of president and CEO of the Peter Drucker Foundation for Nonprofit Management. The Drucker Foundation provides programs and resources to help nonprofits manage themselves more effectively and with a greater emphasis on innovation. Since Frances also serves on many boards and is the recipient of numerous awards, she travels even more often these days than in the past. Far from retiring to the country, she finds that "I haven't been home since taking my new job!"

Barbara Grogan, president and CEO of Western Industrial Contractors, has greatly expanded her field of operations. In addition to opening a branch of her company in Phoenix, Arizona, she and a partner in that city founded a national corporate relocation management company in the spring of 1994. Grogan and Strictland provides office, plant, and family relocation as well as purchasing and liquidating for national clients. "Business," says Barbara, is "booming wildly." In 1992–93, Barbara served as the first woman to chair the board of the Denver Chamber of Commerce. Since stepping down from that, she has been active in a more national arena, devoting time outside her company to the New York–based Committee for Economic Development and to the New American Revolution, an executive group that focuses business on children's issues. She recently bought a cabin in the Rockies and has been able to spend more time traveling since her daughter Holly moved to New York to study acting.

At the time of the diary studies, Dorothy Brunson had just become the first black woman in the United States to purchase an FCC license for an independent television station. Since then, she has concentrated all her energies on building Philadelphia's WGTW-TV "from scratch," starting with the construction of a new facility and moving on to production. Because the new venture took "everything I had in terms of time, energy, and money," Dorothy sold her radio stations in Baltimore and North Carolina and moved her primary residence to Philadelphia, though she kept her Baltimore house and spends time there when she can. In addition to serving as president and general manager of her television station, she also serves as a consultant to banks and venture capitalists looking to invest in broadcast media; she is also a founder of Associated Black Charities. At present, Brunson Communications, Inc., is looking to acquire more television stations. "I'm out of everything else, and onto the information superhighway," Dorothy exults.

Nancy Badore left her fourteen-year career with the Ford Motor Company in 1993 in order to work on her own as a consultant in the field of organizational change. "I'm *very* proud of the work I did at Ford," she says, noting that many members of the new team there are executives with whom she worked directly to change the culture at Ford. She was, however, eager to apply what she had learned at Ford to a broader arena, and now works not only with major companies but also with universities and nonprofits. "Basically, what I like is helping organizations that are serious about charting a course in the midst of turbulent change. I'm doing just what I want and I'm having a grand time." Still living in Dearborn, Michigan, with her husband Peter and her seven-year-old daughter Maggie, she travels extensively but can now adjust her schedule to take Maggie with her to see the world.

The publication of *The Female Advantage* changed my own life quite dramatically. Before the book was published, I had lived a fairly traditional writer's life— working most often in rather lonely isolation. Then suddenly I found myself at the center of a kind of expanding web, in contact with thousands of people all over the country. And over the last five years nationwide, I have spoken at and participated in a variety of—forums with professional women's groups, at universities, in corporations. Being on the circuit can be somewhat draining, but I have also found it nourishing in the extreme. Having a receptive audience is of course gratifying, but even more so is the feeling of being both a witness to and a participant in a process of transformation that is not only shaping a very different kind of workplace but also creating the opportunity for people to build lives that are more satisfying, more creative, more generous, and more whole.

The change in my own career was made much easier because I first had a chance to observe the women profiled in this book. Learning from them enabled me to move with some measure of grace onto a much larger stage. Since I was speaking a lot about leadership, I found myself irrevocably cast in the role of leader as well. Fortunately, I discovered that I had learned a lot about what this means by having spent time with these women.

I had learned above all that leadership demands a fierce belief in your own vision: if what you are trying to build is strong enough, people will want to be associated with your efforts. I also learned that if you need to acquire a certain skill, you must reach out boldly and learn from the very best. For example, since I suddenly found myself doing a lot of public speaking, I sought out the extraordinary coach Joan Kenley in San Francisco. I knew she was right for me when my father serendipitously gave me her book.

Finally, I learned from the women in the diary studies that being both meticulous and prompt in responding to people opens up possibilities at every turn. Both Barbara Grogan and Frances Hesselbein said explicitly that they regarded their correspondence as "an opportunity, not a burden," and they and the other women were disciplined about answering mail and returning phone calls immediately. Since I had made a big point about this in the book, I felt obligated to adopt the same practice, although in the past I had been both sloppy and quick with excuses. And through this effort at self-reform I found my world opening up.

And so I am grateful that I had a chance to observe the women in this book in action before my own life handed me more responsibilities. Inspired by their example, I have been able to meet challenges greater than I could have imagined.

Over the last five years, I have frequently been approached by people who wonder how relevant the leadership skills profiled in *The Female Advantage* are in regard to their own circumstances or positions. "I'm a midlevel manager in my organization," someone will typically say, "and the hierarchy here is still very much in place. I feel a lot in common with the women you studied, and I'd enjoy working more like they do. But I don't know how I can make such use of their style of leading when I don't have all that much power. The women you talked to were heads of their companies—they could do things pretty much as they wanted. Does that mean I have to wait until I'm in a powerful position before I can be true to my own values, and exercise the kind of leadership you talk about in your book?"

I hear some variation on this question everywhere I go. What those who ask do not recognize is that the women in *The Female Advantage* all achieved leadership positions *because* they honored and believed in their own values and skills. When their organizations then entered a period of crisis or change, top management turned to them precisely because their way of doing things was different. Nancy Badore's career offers the clearest illustration of this pattern. The path of the women who left organizations to become entrepreneurs is of course somewhat different.

When reading *The Female Advantage*, therefore, it might be useful to ask yourself how the skills and characteristics the women manifest could work for you in your current circumstances, and what specifically this style could bring to your organization. If, for example, your company is presently configured in such a way that direct communication across levels is taboo, you can still concentrate on creating more open communication within your group or on your team. Efforts at major change always have to start somewhere: why not in you?

Leading in your own way within a small group or unit not only will make you more comfortable and effective but will also position you to assume a greater leadership role when your organization enters a period of crisis that pushes it to be more flexible and responsive—something bound to happen in today's environment. Also, you may find that your group can serve as a sort of customized internal model for what change might look like within your organization. More and more, companies are learning that some of the best new ways of operating come from successful individuals exercising a certain degree of autonomy and leadership within the ranks. It was, in fact, my interest in organizational change as it is occurring at the grassroots level that inspired my new book, *The Web of Inclusion*.

QUESTIONS FOR REFLECTION AND DISCUSSION
The following questions have provided some lively points for discussion in the many gatherings I have led over the past five years.

WOMEN'S WAYS
Is it helpful to think in terms of specific qualities that women leaders bring to organizations? Or might doing so play into reductive stereotypes? If many (though certainly not all!) women are bringing different qualities or attitudes to organizations, what is most likely to account for this? Think about some of the women you've watched who are particularly effective as leaders—in business or in the political arena. What that is new have they brought to the table? How have their methods and styles been perceived by those accustomed to a different approach?

TRANSFORMATION
Women are entering the workplace in substantial numbers and assuming roles of substantial authority for the first time. What long-range effects might this have on our society as a whole—both in the workplace and in family life? Will our culture remain essentially the same in many particulars, or could it be substantially

transformed? Is it possible that the entrance onto the public stage of one half of the human race could *not* be a profoundly transformative event?

BALANCE

The melding of public and private concerns is a theme in *The Female Advantage*. The women leaders profiled in this book see that their public and private concerns are intertwined; they do not, nor do they wish to, compartmentalize their lives, their duties, or their identities. What are the implications of this kind of interpenetration? How can people achieve balance when playing a variety of roles, or trying to meet responsibilities that may seem contradictory? What exactly might balance look like in a less compartmentalized environment?

AUTHORITY.

How do inclusive leaders exercise authority? How do they avoid seeming weak? The women in the diary studies are all confident and strong, but they manifest their strength in ways we are not necessarily accustomed to seeing in organizations. What exactly defines as inclusive leader? How does authority make itself felt in an inclusive organization? As more and more of our organizations change to adapt to very different conditions, will we also begin to change our definition of what constitutes strength in leadership?.

SPORTS

People in organizations have long used metaphors derived from sports in order to describe specific situations and strategies, and the language of winning and losing often prevails. In addition, experience in team sports has long been supposed to be invaluable for shaping organizational leaders. Do you believe sports and games are useful metaphors in the workplace? Do you think experience in sports is helpful in developing leadership? If not, what skills and experiences might contribute more to shaping an effective leader?

STRATEGY

Strategy is usually conceived of as the articulation of specific objectives, and the drafting of a calculated plan to achieve these ends. But in web-like organizations, and among the inclusive leaders profiled in this book, strategy is much more subtle and responsive. The women in the diary studies seem to create strategies by orchestrating strong relationships, which then permit unexpected things to happen. Is the more conventional approach to strategy really limiting, as the leaders profiled here believe? And why might a more intuitive and evolutionary approach be more appropriate to present conditions?

VOICE AND VISION

There is a great emphasis on the importance of vision in today's organizations. But as physicist Evelyn Fox

Keller points out, vision metaphors always imply a separation between the visioner and what he or she envisions; thus the notion of vision fails to acknowledge the profound interconnectedness of all things. Similarly, Carol Gilligan notes that metaphors based on listening and speaking are more likely to reflect the value of interconnectedness and mutuality than those based on seeing. Given this, it is not surprising that a number of the women in this book report that "finding their voice" has been the key to creating their leadership style. Do you feel you have a voice that distinctly reflects what is best in you? If not, what might you do to find that voice?

WARRIORS

Warrior virtues have traditionally defined leadership in the public sphere. But this is beginning to change as we approach the end of the present millennium. Today's technology has allowed us to create weapons that are simply too powerful to be entrusted to those with pure warrior values; in addition, our more interconnected view of life on earth is forcing us to recognize that battles have long-term consequences for us all. What role does the emergence of women onto the public stage play in undermining the traditional view of leader as warrior? What might the archetype of tomorrow's leader look like?

POWER AND POSITION

The women portrayed in this book are leaders in their organizations, with varying degrees of freedom to structure and run things in ways that are comfortable for them. But what if you are *not* in a leadership position: is it still possible to make the best use of your skills, talents, and attitudes if they contradict the way things have typically been done in your organization? Must you wait until you achieve a higher rank before you become a force for positive change? Will there always be a strict correlation between positional power and influence? Are there things you could be doing *now*, within your division or unit, that might help your organization as a whole become more inclusive? My forthcoming book, *The Web of Inclusion,* will deal with strategies that people at a variety of levels have used to bring about change in their organizations. Imagine ways in which you might do the same.

INTRODUCTION

The first seed of this book was planted in the mid-seventies, during a conversation I had with Wenda Wardell Morrone, then features editor at *Glamour* magazine. Over lunch one day, Wenda confided that she had been reading one of those power-and-how-to-get-it books that were being published at the time; popular tomes, written mostly by men, that advised women how to be more like men in order to achieve success in the workplace. All these books assumed that women were not really leaders, shaping organizations or managing people according to their own values; none investigated how women, acting as women, really *led*. They just counseled women on how best to ape what men were doing.

"I don't get it," Wenda lamented. "Everything in the book goes against my own experience! For example, it tells me to keep the people who work for me off-balance and in constant competition. That's supposed to motivate them to work harder. Well, maybe that motivates men, but I've always had women working for me, and if you keep them off-guard, they don't do their best. They get resentful, start procrastinating, and don't feel free to make suggestions. Whereas if you give them support and encouragement, they'll work as hard as they can, really *blossom!*" Wenda concluded that, in her position as manager, she liked to think of herself as a gardener— "watering the flowers, helping them flourish and grow."

The conversation stuck with me. What Wenda said made sense. I knew that *I* worked best when I felt appreciated and secure. When I did not, I tended to put things off, to stew and question. Above all, my imagination seemed to freeze. I could go through the motions of my work, but I couldn't come up with creative solutions or new ideas. The fear of being jumped on or criticized seemed to immobilize my mind.

I had occasion to think about this question of how best to motivate people years later, when I took a job as a speechwriter in a major corporation that was seeking to transform itself from a bureaucratic institution into something sleek and competitive, fashionably "lean and mean." Our speechwriting group was charged with persuading our fellow employees that the company was deeply committed to "culture change," and convincing them that the change would be all for the best—provided they were willing to work like hell and adopt the new "intrapreneurial" values.

We didn't do a very good job, in part because we were caught in the middle, instructed to exalt the new direction while playing by the same old rules. Thus we wrote fiery speeches about the need to blast through bureaucratic barricades—which we then had to submit through the usual bureaucratic layers. But such inconsistencies were not supposed to matter. Our task was to find the right words, words that like magic totems would make people believe in changes they could not see.

And so we devised "mission" and "vision" statements and had them printed up on little plastic cards that people were supposed to carry around in their wallets. We produced glossy broadcasts in which the corporate brass briefed the troops on the new, participative culture. And when internal polls indicated that our fellow employees still weren't buying our message, we crafted threatening speeches, half-time harangues aimed at locker-room losers.

As we floundered, doubts assailed me. Was our essential hypocrisy undermining our message? Surely our fellow employees must have noticed, despite all the tough talk about "cutting to the bone" and "flattening the pyramid," that status perks for the brass remained firmly in place. And might not our negative presumptions, reflected in our threatening tone, be counterproductive in terms of motivating people to work harder? Surveying the situation, I became convinced that our condescending attitude was exacerbating the very cynicism we speechwriters had been hired to combat.

It was then I remembered Wenda Morrone's observation that people don't work well when they don't feel valued, trusted, and respected. I began making this point to the men I worked with, but my views were dismissed as softheaded and softhearted; no more, perhaps, than could be expected of a woman under pressure. But inside me, a conviction was taking root: I believed that I understood what was happening more clearly than the men. And yes, it was partly because I was a woman. For as an outsider unfamiliar with the corporate game, I was more willing to apply what I knew of human nature to my understanding of the situation. And since I was not part of the old culture—was indeed still baffled by its unspoken rules, codes, and presumptions—I could see how old-culture values were undermining the company's stated commitment to change.

Not long afterward, our speechwriting unit was disbanded and let go, a failure, I suppose; unable to find the words which would make people believe that change was real. But I was left with a feeling of excitement, for I had always seen my outsider status as a liability; now for the first time, I recognized that it could be an advantage.

This seemed a startling notion, for I, like many women, had been deeply influenced by books such as Margaret Hennig and Anne Jardim's *The Managerial Woman,* and Betty Lehan Harragan's *Games Mother Never Taught You.* Unlike their crude and presumptuous predecessors—those power-and-how-to-get-it books that had so confounded Wenda Morrone—these books did not urge women to *become* like men in order to achieve workplace success. Rather, they warned us that we had to learn to play the game according to men's rules if we hoped to advance and claim our share in the business world.

Betty Harragan, characterizing business as "a no-woman's-land," urged women to recognize that the modern corporation is structurally modeled on the military, and functions according to the precepts of male team sports.[1] Thus the corporation is an "alien culture," one that women are ill-prepared to understand, having been nurtured on a diet of "sentimental movies and maudlin books." In order to master corporate culture—an "idiot's nightmare" in which "tasks are broken down into dehumanizing fragments"—women must both indoctrinate themselves in the military mind-set ("if it moves, salute it"), and study the underlying dynamic of games such as football.[2] Though women cannot hope to "immediately overcome deficiencies in their upbringing," such preparation will at least enable them to understand and learn to compete in "a world they never made."[3]

The authors of *The Managerial Woman* also urged women to study football, in order to master the male concept of personal strategy. Strategy, as men define it, means "winning; achieving a goal or reaching an objective."[4] Without training in team sports, the authors contend, women get bogged down in "definitions of process; in planning, in finding the best possible way." Seeing a career "as personal growth, as self-fulfillment, as satisfaction, as making a contribution to others, as doing what one wants to do," women lack men's focus on the all-important question, "What's in it for me?"[5] And because they aren't used to playing on a team for a coach, Hennig and Jardim argue, women make the fatal mistake of trying to measure up to their *own* standards, whereas men recognize the need to "center on their bosses' expectations." The authors even commend men for "their larger capacity for dissembling, in the value-free sense of veiling feeling," while women are unfortunately hobbled by their misguided belief that "it is all for real."[6]

Betty Harragan, unlike Hennig and Jardim, does not hold men up as paragons for their mastery of such dubious abilities. Still, she shares with these authors the underlying presumption that women's ways of thinking, doing, and knowing don't have much place in the modern corporation. Harragan does, however, acknowledge that this total domination of male values is not permanent, and guesses that the contemporary bureaucratic model of the corporation "has just about reached the point of no return."[7] Nevertheless, she fully expects that "we are stuck with it for the foreseeable future," and advises women to learn to play the game the way men play it, if only in order "to stay one jump ahead of your adversaries."[8]

Such judgments may have been accurate enough in 1977, when Harragan's book was published, but as we move into the last decade of the twentieth century, we find the workplace radically altered. Pressed by global competition and a fast-changing technology characterized by flexibility and innovation, companies are casting aside old-culture values, trimming the pyramid, and rooting out cumbersome and bureaucratic structures. Even corporations still floundering in these efforts (like the one I worked for), nevertheless recognize that the old chain-of-command hierarchy, with its unspoken rules and codes, is too lumbering and muscle-bound for today's economy.

Of course, it was precisely the old military-hierarchical structure that made women feel least at home; this was the "no-woman's-land" described by Betty Harragan. So it is fortuitous that corporate restructuring is taking place *at the very time* when women are surging into the workplace in record numbers. Driven by the need of most families to earn two incomes, the high divorce rate, and a desire for financial independence, women are planning lifetime careers as never in history. By the end of 1990, they will constitute 45 percent of the labor force. Of female college graduates, 80 percent work, which means participation is greatest at the high end, in positions of authority and influence. Women's share of advanced degrees—in medicine, dentistry, law, accounting, architecture, business and management—is growing fastest of all.[9]

In their fascinating study of corporate change, *Reinventing the Corporation,* John Naisbitt and Patricia Aburdene note, *"Significant change occurs when there is a confluence of changing values and economic neces-*

sity."[10] Both the massive influx of women into the work force and the need for corporate restructuring constitute such a confluence, with each trend spurring, hastening, and reinforcing the other. As companies reinvent themselves, they need to find new structures and values; those that learn from how women do things will have a start. Thus Naisbitt and Aburdene believe that the most successful companies in the future will be those that aggressively hire, train, and promote women. In their words, *"Women can transform the workplace by expressing, not by giving up, their personal values."*[11]

Once I realized that the days of women trying to fit into the corporate mold were over, I saw the need for a new kind of book. Not a book that would tell women what they need to learn about business, but a book about what business can learn from women; a book that would show successful women in action, and demonstrate the effect their leadership is already having on how business is done; a book that would define and reaffirm the values that women recognize as a source of their strength— values that have for too long been dismissed as signs of weakness.

These values include an attention to process instead of a focus on the bottom line; a willingness to look at how an action will affect other people instead of simply asking, "What's in it for me?"; a concern for the wider needs of the community; a disposition to draw on personal, private sphere experience when dealing in the public realm; an appreciation of diversity; an outsider's

xl

impatience with rituals and symbols of status that divide people who work together and so reinforce hierarchies. This is not to say that men do not share these values; some share many, others a few. But these values may be defined as female because they have been nurtured in the private, domestic sphere to which women have been restricted for so long.

There's an old Chinese proverb: *Women Hold Up Half the Sky*. It means that half the work and half the thinking in the world is done by women. For the sky to be complete, both halves must work together; nothing can be truly human that excludes one half of humanity. Until recently, the half of the sky assigned to women has been the private half; the public half has been ceded to men. But as women assume positions of leadership in the public realm, they are bringing their values with them, and the ancient dichotomies—between male and female, between public and private—are dissolving. This book is about what happens when the feminine principles claim their place in the public realm—when women begin to uphold the public half of the sky.

PART I

The Feminine Principles

CHAPTER ONE

Women's Ways of Leading

"I run my company according to feminine principles," proclaims Anita Roddick, founder of The Body Shop, a $300 million international chain of natural cosmetics stores based in London. Anita Roddick defines these feminine principles as "principles of caring, making intuitive decisions, not getting hung up on hierarchy or all those dreadfully boring business-school management ideas; having a sense of work as being part of your life, not separate from it; putting your labor where your love is; being responsible to the world in how you use your profits; recognizing the bottom line should stay at the bottom."[1]

Anita Roddick's description of feminine principles reflects our culture's basic presumptions about the differences between how men and women think and act. We *feel*, many of us, that women are more caring and intuitive, better at seeing the human side, quicker to cut through competitive distinctions of hierarchy and ranking, impatient with cumbersome protocols. Our belief in these notions is intuitive rather than articulated; we back it up with anecdotes instead of argument. Some women feel ashamed of their belief in feminine principles; some are scoffing, others proud, even defiant.

Often, our feelings surface in the form of vague resentments. We're hit with the sudden notion that life would be better if only *we* ran things. An example occurred on the day I first went to interview Anita Roddick in New York. It was a glorious, sunny Saint Patrick's Day, and the streets were thronged with people rejoicing in the last few minutes of their lunch hour. As I turned from the main avenue onto a side street, the ambiance quickly changed. I was swallowed in shadows cast by hulking office towers.

I took the elevator to the forty-first floor of the building where Anita Roddick was waiting, a sprightly woman wearing blue jeans and an oversized white shirt. Leading me into a large, high-windowed office, she gestured to the view of New York's skyline and declared, "Buildings like this are so ridiculous! If women ran the world, we wouldn't have all these ugly phallic towers!"

I felt an impulse to agree with her, and yet I wondered, was there any evidence that she was right? Clearly, Anita Roddick believed that the establishment of feminine principles in the public realm would result in a more humane way of life, but how could we really know if this was true? There were no cities built by women that could be pointed to as evidence. The closest thing we have to women-built cities is women-led organizations.

Studying companies led by women is the best way to

get an answer to that old question, "what would it be like if women ran the world?" And that answer isn't just speculative; it has real importance, for it helps us to understand how our world is evolving, what the world will be like as women come to have more and more impact on the public realm. But in order to gain a clear understanding of this extraordinary change, it is necessary to be very specific. It won't do to resort to generalities about how women run companies, or even rely on their word about how they do it. Rather, the details and nuances of female management must be carefully observed and then compared concretely with how men do things.

In writing this book, then, I have sought to answer the small question before the big ones; to identify the specifics of how women manage before discussing how they are changing the workplace. How do successful women managers make decisions? How do they schedule their days? Gather and disperse information? Motivate their employees? How do they delegate tasks? Structure their companies? Deal with interruptions? Answer mail? Supervise? Hire? Fire? How do their experiences as women—as wives, mothers, friends, sisters, daughters—help or hinder them in developing an effective leadership style? And what is the impact of this style on those around them? Only by looking at such details could I hope to develop a clear definition of feminine principles, and draw a rounded picture of the impact those principles are having in the changing economy.

HOW MEN
MANAGE AND LEAD

In order to know what women managers do differently, I first had to know what male managers do. The definitive answer was not far to seek. In 1968, the management scientist Henry Mintzberg had set out to answer that question. Mintzberg wasn't thinking specifically in terms of men, but since in 1968 the very word *manager* implied a man, the studies he undertook included only men.

The question of what a manager actually does had fascinated Mintzberg since he was a child and had asked his executive father. His father had taken him to the office so he could see for himself. But the young Mintzberg was unable to form any cohesive impression from that experience, beyond noting that his father spent a lot of time on the phone. As a doctoral student, Mintzberg still felt unsatisfied by definitions of a manager's work; he found most of what had been written on the subject to consist of "abstract generalities devoid of the hard data of empirical study."[2] Further, he found that executives themselves often could not explain how the diverse activities that comprised their long and often fragmented days could constitute anything so specific as management.

Determined to identify these tangibles, Mintzberg followed five executives through their days, keeping a minute-by-minute record of their activities. No detail was too insignificant for his scrutiny: when an executive processed mail, how much he talked during meetings, when he skimmed magazines, how he dealt with interruptions, the length of his phone calls. By drawing together this apparent minutiae, Mintzberg was able to discern patterns, to tease out what he called "the design of an executive's working day." And because he used detailed observation, the "hard data of empirical study" instead of generalized analysis, he was able to draw specific conclusions about what managers were doing well, and show how at times they defeated themselves.

The diary studies, as Mintzberg called them, were published in 1968 as a Ph.D. dissertation; in 1973 they became a basis for *The Nature of Managerial Work*. Jeffrey Sonnenfeld, former professor at the Harvard Business School and current director of the Center for Leadership and Career Change at Emory University in Atlanta, described the impact that Mintzberg's work had at the time. "It was completely new. Mintzberg changed the way people looked at management. Before him, the formal aspects had been considered most important— the planning, the organizing, the long-range stuff. The whole picture was very static, emphasizing what a manager *got* accomplished; for example, if he got a labor contract signed. But Mintzberg put the emphasis on what the manager *did* to get that contract, the actual tasks and behaviors, the management by walking around. By focusing on the minute-by-minute, he showed management as fast-moving and reactive, vivid and intense—not programmed at all, but dynamic. That changed the way

9

management schools looked at how we should be training managers. The schools began to see that managers
shouldn't be encouraged to develop themselves as one
thing or another. They had to be many things, wear
different hats, master many skills. They needed a much
richer, more diverse portfolio than we had imagined."[3]

Mintzberg's work provided the description of what a
manager did—a male manager, though at the time this
qualification went unnoted. Among the patterns and similarities he discerned are the following.

1. *The executives worked at an unrelenting pace, with
no breaks in activity during the day.* Nearly 60 percent
of their time was taken up with formal, scheduled meetings. The rest of the time filled up quickly with less
formal encounters based on tasks that required immediate attention. Because of this, the various tasks had
to be performed in rapid succession; consequently, encounters tended to be brief, with half the "events" in
the executive's day lasting less than nine minutes. Mintzberg quotes the Swedish management scientist Sune
Carlson in explaining the flavor of his executives' days.
"All they knew," Carlson wrote, "was that, as managers,
they scarcely had time to start on a new task or sit down
and light a cigarette before they were interrupted by a
visitor or a telephone call." Because of the open-ended
nature of the managers' jobs, tasks expanded to fill available time; as a result, Mintzberg concluded that they
were constantly harassed by "never having the pleasure

of knowing that there was nothing else to do."[4] Even during times when they were supposed to be relaxing, they were continuously plagued by the "nagging suspicion" that something was not getting done.

2. *Their days were characterized by interruption, discontinuity, and fragmentation.* During the course of scheduled meetings, subordinates were always "interrupting"—in one case, to tell of an impending crisis with a public-interest group; in another, to bring news of a fire raging at a plant facility. Thus much of the executives' time was spent "putting out fires"—sometimes literally. This crisis orientation resulted in an interspersing of significant and trivial events that fostered an atmosphere of fragmentation. Free time was constantly being "usurped" by subordinates (the word *usurp,* with its connotations of commandeering and even seizure, figures frequently in descriptions of these executives' days). Because of this perception of constant interruptions, Mintzberg noted that top managers "sought proper protection" from their secretaries, whom they used to "shield" them from the importunings that disturbed the peace of their days.

3. *They spared little time for activities not directly related to their work.* Family time was severely curtailed; Mintzberg noted that many of the executives seemed to regard their homes as "branch offices," places to cram in extra work after hours. Nor did the men have time for outside interests; they rarely went to the theater or

concerts, or read anything that was not directly related to their jobs. As a result, Mintzberg observed that their jobs led to a high degree of intellectual isolation. Their focus was deep, but also extremely narrow.

4. *They exhibited a preference for live action encounters.* Phone calls and face-to-face meetings were the preferred methods of gaining information. As already noted, scheduled meetings consumed nearly 60 percent of their time, which left the executives "preoccupied with diaries and scheduling," always updating and working to devise more efficient systems. Most were impatient with receiving information in written form; a number complained that the processing of their mail was a "burden." As a result, they sought to get through it as quickly as possible, delegating mail-related tasks to their secretaries; Mintzberg expressed surprise that so little time was spent on mail. Periodicals that came into executives' offices were skimmed at an average rate of two per minute. Because they did not consider mail particularly important, they rarely set aside time for the sole purpose of dealing with it.

5. *They maintained a complex network of relationships with people outside their organizations.* Because representing their companies was considered a major aspect of their jobs, between 22 and 38 percent of the executives' time was spent outside the office, primarily in contact with peers, colleagues, and clients. This outside time

functioned as an information-gathering activity, a way of bringing news from the world into the company.

6. *Immersed in the day-to-day need to keep the company going, they lacked time for reflection.* This was one of Mintzberg's key findings. Before his study, as Jeffrey Sonnenfeld noted, management had been considered a matter of planning and organization—a thoughtful enterprise, focused on the long range. Mintzberg's diary studies revealed that in fact executives lacked the leisure for such contemplation. The fast pace and constant interruptions kept them focused on the everyday.

7. *They identified themselves with their jobs.* Because of the all-consuming nature of their work, and the high status it conferred, Mintzberg's men tended to feel that their identity was indistinguishable from their positions. Sitting atop the hierarchical pyramid—for all the organizations they worked in were structured that way—they derived personal prestige from the place they occupied. Mintzberg saw this as presenting a number of problems; among them, the inability to detach. He saw detachment as desirable because the executives performed so many different functions—acting as entrepreneurs, figureheads, decision makers, liaisons. As a result, he believed that executives could benefit from consciously assuming their different roles—putting on different hats, in Jeffrey Sonnenfeld's phrase. Thus a manager exercising his figurehead function would *play* the figurehead role, behaving in a more formal and authoritative man-

ner than when serving as a negotiator or disturbance-handler. But because their personal identities were dependent upon their positions, Mintzberg found his executives unable to summon the playfulness and detachment from their jobs that such a strategy would require.

8. *They had difficulty sharing information.* Sitting at the top of the hierarchical pyramid, Mintzberg's men had extraordinary access to information: from within the company, because all information flows to the top, and from outside the company, because of their extensive network of contacts. This information constituted the chief source of their power, but since they tended to derive their personal identity from the power of their positions, they were reluctant to share the source of that power. The result was a tendency to hoard information, to be more avid to collect than to disseminate it; this was the chief weakness Mintzberg discovered in the managers he studied. Their reluctance to share information caused organizational bottlenecks, and was a prime cause of their overburdened workloads, for it meant that tasks and decisions which could have been made down the line had instead to be resolved at the top.

Along with many neutral descriptive terms that cropped up frequently in Mintzberg's study—*contact, decisional, interpersonal, enterprise*—other frequently used words reflect deeper emotional attitudes: *interruption, usurpation, protection, burden, shield.* These terms give a picture of men who feel pressured by unscheduled and conflicting demands, have a persistent sense of their own importance in the world, and take an instrumental view of others in their organization. In addition, focused on the element of *restriction* implicit in these words, they do not seem open to enjoying the *texture* of their days.

These are rather negative observations, and yet it is important to remember that the five managers Mintzberg studied were all highly successful men, leaders of others as well as of their organizations, who reported being satisfied in their work. Despite the hectic and fragmented pace, and the constant "nagging suspicion" that certain tasks were not being done, they enjoyed the fact of having achieved high-status positions, and took pleasure in the successful accomplishment of so many tasks during a given day. These sources of satisfaction provide a clue as to why the managers felt successful: they were focused on the *completion* of tasks and *achievement* of goals, rather than on the actual *doing* of the tasks themselves. This attitude reveals an instrumental view of their work that mirrors their view of people; that is, the work is a *means* to an *end.*

This observation fits with the contention in *The Managerial Woman* noted in the Introduction, that men tend to define personal strategy in terms of winning, of achieving a goal or reaching an objective.[5] By those standards, Mintzberg's men were hugely fulfilled. They had won the top positions in their organization, and were achieving goals and reaching objectives every day. What might be thought of as problems—an exhausting workload, the sacrifice of family time, the inability to pursue personal development, intellectual isolation, the relentless focus on "putting out fires"—were seen in the context as just part of the cost incurred in the struggle to win the game.

Management consultant Jan Halper confirmed this view in her recent study of male executives, *Quiet Desperation: The Truth About Successful Men.* Halper found that, although 68 percent of senior-level male managers described themselves as happy, more than half of this group also believed that their private life had suffered as a result of their driving pursuit of career success; comments included, "After forty-five years of marriage, I hardly know my wife."[6] Yet more than half of those who said this was true did not regret the number of hours they had spent on the job, and said they would not do things differently if given the chance. In other words, the sacrifice of an active family life was a cost they were willing to pay. Making the sacrifice was not enough to render them unhappy.

HOW WOMEN DIFFER

Mintzberg focused on five men in his diary studies. I chose to focus on four women. To explain why, I must first describe how our books are different. I used Mintzberg's text only to provide me with a method that was both specific and concrete, and to give me a standard of comparison with men. In no way does my book attempt to be a successor to his, or modeled on it; that would be inappropriate to my task, which is not only to describe how women manage companies, but also to define women's impact on the contemporary workplace and, by extension, on the culture as a whole.

In pursuing his purpose, Mintzberg presented his findings almost in the form of lists: the number of letters written, the minutes spent on a telephone call, the approximate length of a meeting. He did not weave these details into a narrative, nor do we ever see his men as characters; we know nothing of their histories, their family situations, what they look like, how they dress, the sound of their voices.

By contrast, I have presented the women I studied as people with personalities and histories. You see and hear them as well as grasp the structure of their days. I felt I had to do this in order to capture not only the details but also the nuances of how they manage, since nuance is so often the key to style. The diary studies in this book are narratives; the women's days tell a story; thus they are quite long, whereas Mintzberg's were extremely short. Since they are long and filled with specifics, I felt it would tax the reader's patience to present five studies merely in order to achieve symmetry with Mintzberg. More important, the four leaders studied represent a variety of work patterns, a range of businesses of vastly different sizes, and different parts of the country as well.

This brings me to a second point. Mintzberg's men were all executives in established corporations; two of the four women I studied were entrepreneurs. Again this choice was deliberate, for it is reflective of the general situation in the United States today. Women are making an enormous contribution as entrepreneurs; fully one third of all new businesses today are started by women, and women are more likely to be top executives in small companies than in large ones.[7] Since my quest was to discover how women are changing the workplace, consideration of this aspect was crucial. Skewing the book in favor of all corporate women would have poorly represented the situation as a whole. I am concerned not with *corporate* women, but with women leaders. In addition, women who own their own companies have a freer hand in setting policy and defining administrative tasks; thus their businesses are especially reflective of women's values.

Further, the general configuration of the business landscape has changed since Mintzberg's studies were published in 1973. America is entering the nineties at a far more entrepreneurial pace. A fast-changing economy that stresses innovation and diversity in order to meet global competition has spawned leaner, less hierarchical organizations and encouraged a flood tide of start-ups. Today's average executive, male or female, is far less likely to be the archetypal "organization man" that in Mintzberg's era was the rule of the day.

Management styles and philosophies have also evolved in response to this general trend—and, as Jeffrey Sonnenfeld has pointed out, in response to work such as Mintzberg's. For this reason, it should be borne in mind that some of the divergences between my findings and Mintzberg's reflect the different decades in which our studies were done more than any differences in how men and women manage. Still, other discrepancies are so striking (and so reflective of differences in male and female psychology noted by researchers like Carol Gilligan[8] and Jean Baker Miller[9]), that they do seem to indicate a basic dissimilarity of approach. Thus comparing elements in the diary studies can help us draw a concrete, empirically based picture of the different ways in which men and women approach the diverse tasks that constitute management. This then can point us to a definition of the feminine principles that is not based on mere speculation, and show us how these principles are being applied in today's workplace.

The following are among the patterns of similarity and dissimilarity I found between the women I studied and Mintzberg's men.

1. *The women worked at a steady pace, but with small breaks scheduled in throughout the day.* Between 40 and

60 percent of their time was spent in formal, scheduled meetings; those in large corporations spent the most time this way. Unscheduled tasks quickly filled what remained of every day: calls to be returned, client follow-ups, brief informal conferences with subordinates and colleagues. The pace was steady and fast, but geared to cause a minimum of frantic stress, partly because the women worked at trying to schedule in very small breaks during the course of the day.

Frances Hesselbein, chief executive of the Girl Scouts, often closed her office door during lunch and read as she relaxed on the sofa; when traveling, she made an effort to arrive the night before her appointments, in order to "have some time to myself." Nancy Badore, director of Ford Motor Company's Executive Development Center, had her secretary leave fifteen-minute breaks between back-to-back meetings when possible, so that she "wouldn't have that desperate feeling of being squeezed." Dorothy Brunson, owner of several radio and television stations, was constantly "snatching at" little pieces of time "so I can just sit and catch my breath." Such deliberate pacing tactics derived from what Barbara Grogan, president of an industrial contracting company in Denver, described as "a recognition that I'm only human and I need my peace of mind."

2. *The women did not view unscheduled tasks and encounters as interruptions.* All four made a deliberate ef-

fort to be accessible, particularly to immediate subordinates. Barbara Grogan used head-high room dividers
instead of walls for her office, "so that people will feel
comfortable popping in." Dorothy Brunson's office wall
was made of glass, "so that everyone can see I'm part
of what's going on." Nancy Badore, as one of the highest
ranking women at Ford, for years maintained an open-
door policy for other women; on the day I was with her,
she let her secretary make a lunch appointment for her
with someone she did not quite remember "because I
think she's some executive's daughter who wants advice." And Frances Hesselbein asks every Girl Scout
employee—"from mailroom to management"—to write
her with suggestions. "It doesn't matter if it's just a
toaster oven for the seventh floor. They need to know
that somebody cares."

Caring. Being involved. Helping. Being responsible.
These were reasons the women in the diary studies gave
for spending time with people who were not scheduled
into their day, and whose concerns may only tangentially
have affected their immediate business. Such encounters
were not regarded as "usurpations" that impeded the
flow of scheduled events, but rather as part of the flow
itself. The difference in the women's view of interruptions from that of Mintzberg's men seemed to stem from
the women's emphasis on keeping relationships in the
organization in good repair, a concern that was reflected
in the words they used. This female focus on relation-

ships was noted in *The Managerial Woman,* though it was perceived by the authors as largely negative. They wrote that women in the workplace tend to "assume without thinking that the quality of relationships is [their] most important priority."[10] This was contrasted in the book with men's supposedly more realistic focus on personal career objectives. But the diary studies reveal that women's concern with relationships gives them many advantages as managers—as will be seen in the following pages.

A final point in regard to interruptions. Because the women accepted them as a normal part of the flow, they did not expect their secretaries to provide them with "proper protection" from the world, as was the case with Mintzberg's men. Rather, they saw their secretaries as conduits who facilitated access to and communication with that world. As Frances Hesselbein remarked, "I'm fortunate to have three secretaries. It means I can keep in contact with more people."

3. *The women made time for activities not directly related to their work.* Although the open-ended nature of their jobs certainly demanded long hours, none permitted this to mean the sacrifice of important family time, or time to broaden their understanding of the world. Frances Hesselbein, a widow with a grown son, did say that her work consumed her life, but she characterized this as a conscious choice and said she had not permitted the same degree of absorption when her family was still living with her. Nancy Badore, the mother of a two-

year-old, was strict about her hours; she came into the office at 8:30 (late by Ford's standards), and tried to make sure she was out by 6:00, so that she and her husband could enjoy evenings with their child. Barbara Grogan, divorced and with two school-aged children, never went into the office on weekends, and discouraged her employees from doing so because "they have families too." She summed up the prevailing view when she declared that her family life did not suffer because it was her *priority;* given a conflict, "I always put my children first." She was willing to put off work-related tasks that did not demand immediate attention in order to prevent business responsibilities from infringing on family time.

In addition, none of the women appeared to suffer from the intellectual isolation that Mintzberg noted among the men. In no case did a woman restrict her reading to material that related only to her work. Frances Hesselbein and Dorothy Brunson (whose two sons are in college) both characterized themselves as voracious readers, consuming books on history, management, and current events, as well as occasional novels or mystery stories. Nancy Badore reads "every magazine from *Vanity Fair* to the *National Enquirer,*" in order to keep current; both she and Dorothy Brunson study and collect art. Barbara Grogan devours "psychology and spiritual books" at night when she goes to bed, in order to keep herself on a "positive track." As Frances Hesselbein explained, "Everything I read relates in some way to managing the Girl Scouts. If it just broadens my understanding of the world, that helps."

4. *The women preferred live action encounters, but scheduled time to attend to mail.* They were similar to Mintzberg's men in their preference for dealing with people by telephone, or in brief, unscheduled meetings, but different in that none appeared to view her mail as a "burden." Nancy Badore reserved an hour every other day to go through it with her secretary; she dictated responses while the secretary took shorthand. Frances Hesselbein used a dictating machine to compose a constant stream of letters between meetings; she prided herself on answering every letter she received within three days, and asked everyone in her organization to do the same. Barbara Grogan wrote personal notes on yellow pads by hand, then gave them to her secretary to type. "I have to scratch around, or it doesn't sound like me," she explained. The women's greater patience with the mail seemed to stem from their view of it as providing a way of keeping relationships in good repair by being polite, thoughtful, and personal.

5. *They maintained a complex network of relationships with people outside their organizations.* In this, they were no different than Mintzberg's men. They considered representing their companies a major aspect of their jobs, and spent between 20 and 40 percent of their time with clients, peers, and colleagues.

6. *They focused on the ecology of leadership.* Mintzberg noted that his men tended to become overly absorbed in the day-to-day tasks of management, and so rarely had time to contemplate the long range. This was not true of the women, who kept the long term in constant focus. For example, Dorothy Brunson monitored radio stations for at least two hours a day in whatever city she found herself: "I'm always looking at what people are doing, at what's going on. Every single trend that happens in this country has an effect on broadcasting."

However, as Frances Hesselbein points out, both male and female managers tend to be more big-picture oriented today than in Mintzberg's era, as a result of the advent of a global economy. What distinguishes the women's view of the big picture, however, is that it encompasses a vision of society—they relate decisions to their larger effect upon the role of the family, the American educational system, the environment, even world peace. This broad focus derives from their consciousness of themselves as participants in a revolution in expectations of and opportunities for women. This social dimension gives resonance to their view of the world and the importance of their place in it; they feel they must make a difference, not just to their companies, but to the world. This evidence of the women's big-picture thinking contradicts conventional wisdom about differences in how men and women manage. But much of what has been written on the subject has been based on comparisons between male CEOs and women in supervisory positions far down the ladder, rather than women in comparable leadership roles.[11]

7. *They saw their own identities as complex and multi-faceted.* Unlike Mintzberg's men, who identified themselves with their positions, the women viewed their jobs as just one element of who they were. Other aspects of their lives simply took up too much time to permit total identification with their careers. "Raising two kids alone, how could I forget that I'm a mom *and* a manager?" asked Barbara Grogan. Being less identified with their careers permitted the women a measure of detachment. Nancy Badore: "Having a baby gives you a sense of what's really important. You still work like hell, but it's all in perspective."

Mintzberg noted that their *lack* of detachment made it difficult for the men he studied to consciously adopt various roles. They had a hard time playing whatever part was called for—figurehead, liaison, negotiator—because they identified too strongly with the position as a whole. The women were clearly more able to do this. "Sometimes, it's like I'm in a play," said Barbara Grogan. "I have different roles with different scripts, but *I'm* the same person. It's the same actress in those parts." Dorothy Brunson went so far as to keep two side-by-side offices in order to strengthen her sense of playing different roles. "In this little office, I wear my general manager's hat," she explained, standing behind one of her two desks. "I'm less important when I'm in here. In my big office, I can be more corporate." Brunson also took joyous relish in playing different parts with clients, bankers, and employees—whatever was called for at the moment. With some, she was the strict but concerned mother; with others, the savvy deal maker; with yet others, the wise and experienced leader. The process was very conscious. "It's not as if I'm different people. I'm just playing up different parts of who I am."

8. *The women scheduled in time for sharing information.* Whereas Mintzberg's men tended to hoard information, the women structured their days to include as much sharing as possible; it was a deliberate process, a major goal of every day. Frances Hesselbein invited employees to sit in her office and watch while she performed various tasks, such as giving telephone interviews. Dorothy Brunson met with a group of very young disc jockeys in order to get their input and share her thinking when she was confronted with a major format change at one of her stations. In her memorable phrase: "I see myself as a transmitter—picking up signals from everywhere, then beeping them out to where they need to go."

Again, this impulse to share information seemed to derive from the women's concern with relationships. Lots of give-and-take kept the network in good repair. Sharing was also facilitated by their view of themselves as being in the center of things rather than at the top; it's more natural to reach *out* than to reach *down*. They tended to structure their companies as networks or grids instead of hierarchies, which meant that information flowed along many circuits, rather than up and down in prescribed channels (more on this in Chapter 2). And since Mintzberg found that hoarding information added significantly to his executives' workloads, the women's willingness to share enabled them to keep their jobs from gobbling precious family and private time.

The characteristics of the women in the diary studies strongly interrelate with and reinforce one another. Their willingness to share information derived from a complex sense of their own identity, which enabled them to keep their careers in perspective. This broad sense of identity in turn encouraged a big-picture focus—on the *world* rather than just the organization—which was strengthened by the women's participation in activities that had nothing to do with their jobs. The scheduling of breaks into the day helped relieve the kind of pacing that can make unscheduled events seem like crises or interruptions. Being attentive to the mail was a way of sharing information.

The interrelation of these attitudes and qualities is reflected in the words the women use: *flow, interaction, access, conduit, involvement, network, reach.* These are words that above all emphasize relationships with people; they are also *process* words that reveal a focus on the doing of various tasks rather than on the completion.

A picture emerges from the diary studies of women who do not take an instrumental view of either work or people—that is, neither is simply the means to achieving the end of a certain position; both are rather ends in themselves.

REASONS FOR
THE DIFFERENCES

Mintzberg's men, judged by their own ends-over-means standards, were highly successful. They held power, controlled information, made decisions, represented their companies, allocated resources, had authority and status; they had achieved their strategic objectives by reaching the very top of their respective fields. Yet in comparison with the women I studied—in the ways I have outlined— they often come off as less reflective and deliberate, narrower. Is it possible that I am stacking the deck in the women's favor? Judging them on their strengths and the men on their weaknesses?

I don't think so. There are specific reasons why the women in the diary studies have certain advantages in their ability to communicate, to prioritize, to see the broad picture. As mentioned before, the different eras in which the studies were conducted have everything to do with the way the women and men are perceived.

Mintzberg's men were managing their companies in the days when, in Betty Harragan's phrase, corporations were still "strictly male cloning productions."[12] The organizations the men headed were hierarchically structured along the old military chain-of-command principle; having worked their way up through rigidly defined channels, the men naturally reflected their company's values. In those days, managers tended to stay with the company they started with, and this focus on security and loyalty made the "organization man" the archetypal figure of his era. Value was placed on narrow expertise (the sixties were the great age of the expert); on the mastery of prescribed skills; and on conformity to the corporate norm.

Today's organizations are very different. The hierarchical structure has given way in innovative companies to the lattice or the grid—less formal structures that deemphasize chain of command and seek to identify managerial talent in less rigid ways. The whole economy is more diverse; new ventures start up quickly; many talented men and women change companies every few years. The focus is on innovation and fast-paced informational exchange; cumbersome channels are looked on as counterproductive. Value is placed on breadth of vision, on what Jeffrey Sonnenfeld called a "diverse portfolio of skills," and on the ability to think creatively. The underlying mentality of our time is *ecological*, stressing the interrelatedness of all things. These are increasingly the values of today's reinvented corporation, and the women in the diary studies, as our contemporaries, share them.

Yet even accounting for this, the women may still be better managers than Mintzberg's men. Since a far smaller percentage of women than men make it to the top, it makes sense that the women who do would more likely be of a higher quality. According to studies done from a wide database at the Center for Values Research (CVR) in Dallas, top women managers are more likely to be what the center characterizes as "existential" leaders—that is, leaders who are able to reconcile a concern for bottom-line results with a concern for people; who focus on both ends and means; who are good at both planning and communication; and who are "reality-based," able to comprehend all the important aspects of *existence*—thus the term "existential."[13] CVR estimates that this is so because a fiercer weeding-out process takes place among women managers; those who do survive must be the very best. Also, CVR has found that co-workers tend to be more hostile and negative toward women managers who lack human relations skills, which prevents women not strong in these skills from reaching positions of authority and influence.

Other reasons that the women in the diary studies appear to be better managers include the experiences and expectations they bring to the workplace. The experiences include their active involvement in the domestic sphere. Increasingly, motherhood is being recognized as an excellent school for managers, demanding many of the same skills: organization, pacing, the balancing of conflicting claims, teaching, guiding, leading, monitoring, handling disturbances, imparting information. The women in the diary studies agreed that their experience as mothers had been valuable. As Barbara Grogan put it, "If you can figure out which one gets the gumdrop, the four-year-old or the six-year-old, you can negotiate any contract in the world."

The women saw themselves as having no choice but to be actively involved in the domestic sphere; motherhood was not a responsibility that could be ducked. Unlike the men in Mintzberg's studies, they had no wives who could shield them from family problems; three of the four had no husbands living at home, which does not make them unrepresentative of the general situation.[14] As a result, the women had every incentive to learn to balance conflicting demands. They achieved this in part by placing firm limits on time spent at work, and in part by integrating the public and private aspects of their lives. Over and over, the women in the diary studies talked about how their lives were "all of a piece," how "everything—home and work—just flows together." As Nancy Badore explained, "I compartmentalize nothing! I'm the same person at work as I am at home. What you see is exactly what you get. That feeling of wholeness unlocks my reserves, gives me a lot of energy. I don't think people who box their lives off in little pieces can *do* as much." Frances Hesselbein agreed. "What exhausts a person is not hard work, but the strain of feeling compartmentalized, limited, cut off, boxed in."

The integration of home and work was reflected in the

diary studies by the women's mental involvement with their families during the workday. They called home, talked to children, housekeepers, and caretakers, occasionally they even noted chores relating to family on their office calendars. By contrast, none of Mintzberg's men appeared to spend *a single moment* dealing with family issues.[15] The men seemed to exist solely as managers when they were on the job; it was as if their fatherhood and husbandhood existed in a vacuum. Their identities had been tightly compartmentalized.

The need to integrate workplace and private sphere responsibilities made the women's lives more complex, but also gave them a certain advantage. Those in the diary studies simply had no choice but to become well-integrated individuals with strong psychological and spiritual resources in order to wrest what they sought from life. Mintzberg's men, deprived of this demanding imperative, developed into less rounded individuals, more subject to the human and intellectual alienation that makes the workplace, and life itself, sterile.

This alienation leads to the "quiet desperation" that Jan Halper found characterized many successful men. Although the majority saw their sacrifice of family and personal time as the inevitable cost of success, and claimed they would not do things differently if given a chance, they nevertheless confessed to deep feelings of emptiness, pointlessness, and resentment, a dissatisfaction that, though vague and inarticulated, was also profound.[16] Having done what was expected of them, and given up everything else, they had not paid attention to their particular goals or dreams, and so were *unaware* of what they really wanted. The women in the diary studies, of course, had *not* done what was expected, so the paths they carved out for themselves were more truly theirs. They were more likely, in Joseph Campbell's memorable phrase, to be "following their bliss"[17]—living their lives out of their own authentic center. Doing so would enhance the feeling of personal wholeness to which the women attributed the unlocking of their energies.

Women's expectations also played a role in preparing them to be outstanding managers. As already noted, the women in the diary studies did not consider their pace to be unbearably hectic; nor did they tend to view unscheduled encounters and calls as interruptions. As Barbara Grogan explained, "I don't think in terms of interruption. When something unexpected needs my attention, it just goes to the top of my list. Maybe that comes from being a mom. If a kid suddenly has to go to the doctor, that isn't an interruption—that's a priority! As a mother, you find there's always something new to be fitted in. You learn not to expect to ever completely control your schedule."

The old adage may be at work here. Men are raised expecting their work to last from "sun to sun," while women know their kind of work will never be done. As Diana Meehan, head of The Institute for the Study of Men and Women at the University of Southern California, observes, "All over the world, women's work is essentially cyclical and unending; the tasks are not the kind that lend themselves to closure. And it's not just child-raising. The difference goes back to the organization of hunter-gatherer societies. The men get together and go out for the occasional big kill, a specific event that has a climax, and then it's over. But the women, who plant and gather, work at continuous tasks that need to be done again and again. This leads them to have more of a *process* orientation; and when you focus on process rather than on achievement or closure, you get more satisfaction from the work itself. You get pleasure from the actual *doing* of it, rather than from the abstract notion of getting it done."[18]

THE FEMININE PRINCIPLES

Since the mid-seventies, when women began entering the workplace in substantial numbers and attempting to "climb up through the ranks," there has been a widespread presumption that their progress is being hampered because so few grew up playing competitive team sports. Such sports, football in particular, have long been viewed as an informal training ground for business leaders, and many books for women seeking workplace success have urged that they learn the fundamentals of the game—study a good diagram and spend a few Sunday afternoons in front of the TV.

Football was assumed to parallel business in a number of specific ways: its organizational structure, its tenacious focus on objective, its obsession with blocking the competition, its emphasis on the deployment of efficient units, and its need for team players who do what they're told and do not question the coach. Michael Novak, in *The Rise of the Unmeltable Ethnics*, described football as providing a "paradigm of professionalism," which he defined as "the remaking of human beings in the image of machines."[19] Football phrases and language are part of business jargon: fumblers drop the ball or miss the play; real competitors feint, run with it, and punt if they need to hedge; they play by the rules, and don't step out of bounds. Even the financial reward of business success, money, is often one-dimensionally described as "just a way of keeping score." But above all, football has been imagined to reflect business's underlying ethos, best expressed in the immortal aphorism attributed to Vince Lombardi: "Winning isn't everything, it's the *only* thing."

But football is not business. As Betty Harragan points out, business is a mental game that bears no resemblance to "a bunch of male brutes" crashing around on Astroturf. Many men would *like* business to be football, so they could feel a kinship with their gridiron heroes, but using football language does not make it so. And the metaphors of football, if they ever applied, have become irrelevant in today's reinvented corporation, which Naisbitt and Aburdene describe as "an environment for nurturing personal growth," a place in which "top-down authoritarianism is yielding to a networking style, and where everyone is a resource for everyone else."[20] That doesn't sound much like football.

Much of the literature that exalts team sports as providing good preparation for business also derides girls' games as useless for this purpose.[21] Turn-taking games such as hopscotch and jump rope are scorned as particularly pathetic, since they emphasize cooperation over competition and have simple and fluid rules that participants may reformulate as desired. Girls who go into business are widely believed to have wasted childhood hours in activities that stress role-playing—playing house or hospital, or devising scenarios for their dolls. Yet the diary studies reveal that an ability to self-consciously adopt various roles is an asset in handling the diverse tasks of management. In addition, games without elaborate rules foster improvisational skills, and reformulating rules to fit situations teaches flexibility. Finally, games that teach cooperation help one to function in organizations where networking provides the structure. Thus girls' games *do* instill skills and attitudes that have value in the workplace—particularly in today's workplace, where innovation, entrepreneurship, and creativity are in demand, and the authoritarian chain of command is increasingly obsolete.

As Carol Gilligan points out in her brilliant study of female developmental psychology, *A Different Voice*, children's games enable them to resolve pressing emotional issues—issues that are very different for each sex.[22] Since girls, identifying with their mothers, feel threatened by separation, they are anxious to preserve relationships; thus their games place a high ethical value on cooperation and being responsible toward others. By contrast, boys, eager *not* to identify with their mothers, feel threatened by intimacy, and anxious to preserve their autonomy. Thus their games place a high ethical value on defining rules and boundaries, and adjudicating disputes that arise from the clash of competing rights. As a result of these differences, it is ridiculous to argue that girls are handicapped by not having played competitive team sports, since such sports, as Gilligan points out, serve no vital purpose in female development.[23]

In addressing the different needs of boys and girls— the different psychological tasks they face—the kinds of games they play help to form them into very different human beings. Male children learn to put winning ahead of personal relationships or growth; to feel comfortable with rules, boundaries, and procedures; and to submerge their individuality for the greater goal of the game. Females learn to value cooperation and relationships; to disdain complex rules and authoritarian structures; and to disregard abstract notions like the quest for victory if they threaten harmony in the group as a whole.

And so a picture of "feminine principles" emerges that is remarkably close to Anita Roddick's spontaneous definition: "principles of caring, making intuitive decisions, not getting hung up on hierarchy or all those dreadfully boring business-school management ideas; having a sense of work as being part of your life, not separate from it; putting your labor where your love is; being responsible to the world in how you use your profits; recognizing the bottom line should stay there—at the bottom."

These feminine principles had little chance for influence in the days when corporations were still "strictly male cloning productions," in Betty Harragan's words; when "the ideas, brains, and creative instincts of women had no part in fashioning our society's organizations."[24] But corporations have changed rapidly since then, driven by fast-changing technologies, global competition, the shortage of skilled labor, and the need to adjust to a diverse work force that includes a large percentage of women. They are reinventing themselves to accommodate a wider focus, to foster creativity and nurture new ideas—simply in order to survive. Thus they are finding common ground with the values that women have been raised and socialized to hold, the values that underlie the feminine principles.

So a confluence exists. What business needs now is exactly what women are able to provide, and at the very time when women are surging into the work force. But perhaps even more important than work force numbers is the fact that women—who began this sweeping entry in the mid-seventies—are just now beginning to assume positions of leadership, which give them the scope to create and reinforce the trends toward change. The confluence is fortunate, an alignment that gives women unique opportunities to assist in the continuing transformation of the workplace—"by expressing, not by giving up, their personal values."[25]

CHAPTER TWO

The Web
of Inclusion

Far into the night, while the other creatures slept, Charlotte worked on her web. First she ripped out a few of the orb lines near the center. She left the radial lines alone, as they were needed for support. As she worked, her eight legs were a great help to her. So were her teeth. She loved to weave, and she was an expert at it.

—*Charlotte's Web*
E. B. White

It is lunchtime in the pink-and-green garden dining room of the Cosmopolitan Club in upper Manhattan, the all-women's club started by Abigail Rockefeller when the Union, her husband's club, refused to serve her. The atmosphere is genteel, with stone planters trailing petunias and women mostly over fifty, some even wearing hats with veils.

It seems an unlikely place in which to be discussing modern leadership and management techniques, but I am with Frances Hesselbein, chief executive of the Girl Scouts, a woman who bridges the paradox with ease. With her low, well-disciplined voice, Hermès scarf and bag, and grooming so perfect you expect that, like the

Duchess of Windsor, she must polish the soles of her shoes, Frances Hesselbein clearly belongs to the world represented by the Cosmopolitan Club. Yet she is also the woman who brought modern management to her organization with such success that Peter Drucker called her "perhaps the best professional manager in America."

I am attempting to interview her, despite the club's rather archaic ban on "visible paper"; apparently ladies are not to engage in business over lunch. So I am balancing my notebook on my knees under a napkin and scribbling without looking while an elderly waitress serves Parker House rolls with silver tongs. Frances Hesselbein is describing the management structure she devised for the Girl Scouts, a replacement for the old hierarchical pyramid.

The new system is circular, she explains; positions are represented as circles, which are then arranged in an expanding series of orbits. "I use circles," she says, "because symbolically they are important. The circle is an organic image. We speak of the *family* circle. The circle is *inclusive*, but it allows for flow and movement; the circle doesn't box you in! I've always conceived of management as a circular process. When I was head of my regional organization, I devised a structure similar to the one I'm using now. It wasn't something I'd read I should do, it was just something I felt. These days, there are all these theories about the circular management model, but with me it was intuitive—this attraction I've always had to the circle."

Suddenly, Frances Hesselbein seizes a wooden pepper mill and sets it in the middle of our table. "This is me," she says, "in the center of the organization." She moves a glass of iced tea and several packets of sugar to form a circle around the pepper mill. "And this is my management team, the first circle." Using cups and saucers, Frances Hesselbein constructs a second circle around the first. "These are the people who report to the first team. And beyond this outer circle, there's another, and another beyond that. And they're all interrelated." She picks up knives and forks and begins fashioning radials to link up the orb lines. "As the circles extend outward, there are more and more connections. So the galaxy gets more *interwoven* as it gets bigger!"

The table at the Cosmopolitan Club is a mess, but I am fascinated. Frances Hesselbein has created the perfect image of a spider's web. And the image of the web has been haunting me lately, for I have been thinking about structure. More specifically, about how women structure things differently from men—companies, office spaces, human relationships, even their own presumed place in the universe.

THE WEB AS STRUCTURE

While doing the diary studies, I became aware that the women, when describing their roles in their organizations, usually referred to themselves as being in the middle of things. Not at the top, but in the center; not reaching down, but reaching out. The expressions were spontaneous, part of the women's language, indicating unconscious notions about what was desirable and good. Inseparable from their sense of themselves as being in the middle was the women's notion of being connected to those around them, bound as if by invisible strands or threads. This image of an interrelated structure, built around a strong central point and constructed of radials and orbs, quite naturally made me think of a spider's web—that delicate tracery, compounded of the need for survival and the impulse of art, whose purpose is to draw other creatures to it.

The image of the web not only imbued the language of the women in the diary studies; it was also evident in the management structures they devised, and in the way they structured their meetings. Frances Hesselbein's "circular management chart," drawn with cutlery and sugar packets, was the most obvious example, and perhaps the most fully articulated. Jokingly called the Girl Scouts' "Wheel of Fortune" by Peter Drucker, the wheel actually *spins;* most management staff jobs are rotated every two or three years. Frances Hesselbein explains that job rotation used in conjunction with the circular chart is ideal for team-building. Teams can be formed to address needs as they arise—for example, the devising of an eighteen-month plan—then disbanded once the task has been accomplished. People serve both on different teams and in different positions, which offers staff people wide experience in the organization. In addition, being rotated into different jobs instills a feeling of common enterprise, cuts down on the tendency to form cliques and fiefdoms, and helps managers understand firsthand both the difficulties that face and the priorities that drive their fellows. "But the reason we have such team-building freedom is because of our circular chart," says Frances Hesselbein. "When someone gets shifted, he or she is simply moved around or across—it doesn't feel like a demotion because there is no up or down. There's no onus attached to being moved."

Nancy Badore's entire career has been built on the notion that management is best done by interrelating teams; she helped to develop the model for training Ford's top executives in this style on the factory floor, and then brought it, to the chagrin of some, to the executive suite. She runs the Executive Development Center along participatory lines; the management chart shows her in the center, with team members (who head the various programs for executives) branching out like the arms of a tree, rather than in a wheel configuration. Her monthly team meetings, at which the program managers make their progress reports, are not, she explains, "about them reporting to *me*. They're about *them* getting exposure to one another's projects and ideas." Thus she appears not so much to be chairing the meeting, but acting as facilitator, extracting and directing information. This is very much like Dorothy Brunson's view of her role as "a transmitter," absorbing information, then beaming it out "to wherever it needs to go."

47

Similarly, when Barbara Grogan chairs a meeting of the governor of Colorado's Small Business Advisory Council (which she had founded), she focuses attention on encouraging the participants to exchange ideas with one another, and forge new alliances among themselves. She describes the process of using her central position to promote interchange as "encouraging the flow," echoing Frances Hesselbein's language.

Implicit in such structurings is the notion of group affiliation rather than individual achievement as having the highest value. This emphasis was obvious in the ways the women described their notions of success. "I never wanted success if it meant clawing my way over other bodies," said Barbara Grogan. "I always knew that would make it pretty lonely once I got there." Frances Hesselbein expressed a similar notion. "I don't have the pressure on me that people have who think of themselves as being out there alone. I think of myself as part of a long continuum. That continuum includes my family, but also all of the fifty-six million women who have ever been in the Girl Scouts—a long green line going back in time and giving me support. Thinking of yourself as part of something larger frees you. You don't feel this sense of individual burden. It's been the source of so much of my energy."

The web of concern may be very large, as Nancy Badore notes. "The Executive Development Center trains Ford executives all over the world, so I try to think in global terms. I don't just see Ford as this company, an entity unto itself; it's a piece of the world, interrelated by politics, history, and economics. And I'm part of that. So while I'm asking myself what role the company can play, I'm also asking what role I can play, particularly as a woman. I'm asking it in terms of the world: where can I make my best contribution? The question really gets down to *why was I born?*"

Thus thinking in terms of the larger group is an important component of the "ecological" focus that I found among the women in the diary studies. This enlarged consciousness derives in part from the women's awareness of themselves as women, in the vanguard of a movement that is changing history. Thus a kind of hidden agenda informs their actions and decisions, manifesting itself as a mission both to improve the status of women and change the world.

This sense of having a larger concern—a concern for the group or whole—is of course implicit in the imagery of the web. The orb and radial lines bind the whole together; every point of contact is also a point of connection. The principle, as Frances Hesselbein observed about the circle, is *inclusion.* You can't break a web into single lines or individual components without tearing the fabric, injuring the whole.

FROM HIERARCHY TO WEB

Carol Gilligan, in *A Different Voice*, consistently opposes the image of the hierarchy to that of the "web of connection" in describing the difference between what women and men view as valuable in this world. She writes, "The images of hierarchy and web, drawn from the texts of men's and women's fantasies and thoughts, convey different ways of structuring relationships, and are associated with different views of morality and self."[1] She notes that these images are in their way mirror opposites, because *the most desirable place in the one is the most feared spot in the other.* "As the *top* of the hierarchy becomes the *edge* of the web, and as the *center* of the network of connection becomes the *middle* of the hierarchical progression, each image marks as dangerous the place which the other defines as safe."[2] In the hierarchical scheme of things, "reaching the top"—where others cannot get close—is the ultimate goal; in the web, the top is too far from the center. The ideal center spot in the web is perceived in the hierarchical view as "being stuck" in the middle—going nowhere.

The contrasting models also reveal different notions of what constitutes effective communications. Hierarchy, emphasizing appropriate channels and the chain of command, discourages diffuse or random communication; information is filtered, gathered, and sorted as it makes its way to the top. By contrast, the web facilitates direct communication, free-flowing and loosely structured, by providing points of contact and direct tangents along which to connect.

The women in the diary studies, eager to be "in the center of things" and chilled by the notion of being "alone at the top," echo the values, principles, and presumptions that Carol Gilligan found to be characteristic of women in general, that indeed she believed to be structured into the female psyche. These values have long been restricted to the private sphere, but that is dramatically changing; the women in the diary studies, having attained positions of authority and influence in the public realm, are able to structure their principles into the way they do business. Thus, using the model of the web to design management charts and apportion office space, to construct meetings and evolve more direct means of communication, they are participating in an *institutionalizing of the web.*

In *Re-inventing the Corporation,* Naisbitt and Aburdene propose the lattice or grid as the structural model for the new corporate economy.[3] It is interesting to note that these structures, with their interconnecting points and intersecting lines, are quite similar to the web—except that they are bound by boxlike shapes rather than circles. Thus the structure of the reinvented corporation is far closer to the female perception of what is desirable, though it retains an essential "male" angularity. The grid of interlocking pieces facilitates direct communication, can shift to meet changing demands, and hastens the flow of information. The image recalls that of the microchip—making quick connections, breaking information into bits, processing, rearranging the units: energy moving in pulses rather than being forced to run up and down in channels.

51

Such a model is obviously more suited to the information age than the hierarchical structure, which found its most widespread application in the industrial era.[4] Yet hierarchical concepts have continued to influence institutional structures because they represent a particular manifestation of male psychology, meeting male needs for limits and boundaries on relationships in the workplace, and satisfying the male value for ends over means. But as women continue to assume positions of influence in the public sphere, they are countering the values of the hierarchy with those of the web, which affirms relationships, seeks ways to strengthen human bonds, simplifies communications, and gives means an equal value with ends.

THE POINT OF AUTHORITY IN THE WEB

When organizations are structured in a top-to-bottom chain of command, lines of authority are extremely clear. The old "if it moves, salute it" mentality prevails. But how does authority manifest itself when the head of an organization sees herself as being at its center? How does a manager in her various roles as information gatherer, decision maker, planner, figurehead, and information disseminator exert authority from the fixed point at the center of the web?

First, it must be noted that, although lines of authority in a web structure may appear diffuse, even tangled, the women in the diary studies are very much the leaders in their organizations, the ones upon whom final responsibility rests. All could be characterized as strong leaders: they have vivid personalities, are direct, and, most important, have specific visions of where they wish to lead and the methods they must use to achieve their goals. Nor are their organizations run as participatory democracies, with everyone contributing in a haphazard way. The women are authorities as much as if they sat at the very top of a hierarchical ladder, but that authority has more subtle ways of manifesting itself.

A prime example is in information-gathering. In a top-down management, information flows upward through channels; authority is established by having access to this progressively filtered information. The chain of command is broken, however, if the authority bypasses established channels in order to ask direct questions down the ladder. By contrast, being at the center, connected to every point in the whole, makes it possible to gather information directly from all sources. Frances Hesselbein made it a practice to receive and answer herself any suggestions made by any member of the 500-person paid staff, whether an accountant or mailroom employee. The most important aspect of this direct contact was that there was no filter, no supervisory layer through whom "lower-downs" were expected to go.

In regard to decision-making, the manager operating from the center of the web can use this direct access to information not only to widen input, but to test reception to decisions in advance. Both these benefits give the decision maker more data when making a decision, but do not dilute the necessity for the *leader* to make it; diffuse lines do not mean fuzzy decisions. Dorothy Brunson, meeting with her young disc jockeys to get their input on a decision, could also solicit their views of how her decision would impact their listeners and the way in which they programmed their shows, and get their reactions on different options she was considering. She described the process: "I never make hasty decisions. The main thing is to cast a wide net, look in many directions, seek a lot of information. Then I maybe take a walk in the evening, let the information jell. And when I make my decision, that's *it*."

In terms of planning for the future, the process of leading from the center of the web is very subtle, and derives its strength from nourishing and fortifying the bonds between intersecting points. In Frances Hesselbein's management team meeting, when conflict arose over issues relating to future plans, she asked the antagonists to work out a plan between themselves and then bring it to her for discussion—which of course implied that the final judgment would be hers. But handling the conflict in this way assured her that the plan the team members devised would meet the requirements of both their departments, while also helping them forge tighter bonds to strengthen the fabric of the organization as a whole. Further, because her circular management chart eliminates ups and downs as well as layers, Frances

Hesselbein was able to invite the antagonists to work things out among themselves without regard to who was above or below whom in rank.

Figurehead authority derives in top-down management from being literally the *head;* it manifests itself as power to set an organization's vision, to represent it in the world. In a web construction, the figurehead is the *heart* rather than the head, and so does not need layers and ranks below to reinforce status. Authority comes from connection *to* the people around rather than distance *from* those below; this in itself helps to foster a team approach. In acting as a figurehead, the leader with a web conception need not insist on rank, authority, and importance in order to convincingly represent the organization. This can be an effective disarming technique, as when Barbara Grogan, at the Governor's Small Business Advisory Council meeting, was able in effect to trumpet her company's latest success and at the same time underplay it by including others in her success: "Can you imagine, our little consulting branch is actually real! Now we're all on our way!"

As a disseminator of information, the leader who operates from the center of the web has the same advantages as when in an information-gathering role. She has direct access to anyone within the organization without having to resort to channels, and thus avoids the attendant risks of dilution and distortion. Further, because releasing information does not lessen authority in the web (as happens in the top-down structure whenever information flows *down),* that information can function as a tool to draw people together.

As mentioned, Nancy Badore made a point of structuring her monthly meetings with the managers who devised programs for the EDC *"not* in order for them to report to me, but so that they can have a chance to share what they're doing, feed off one another's ideas, know exactly what is going on." Again, the concept of strengthening ties is most important; the leader at the center derives strength from building up connections rather than from compartmentalizing, dividing in order to conquer. There is nothing to be gained by restricting the flow of information to the top—hoarding it, as Mintzberg noted his men were wont to do.

There is an aspect of teaching that accompanies authority as it flows from the center of the web. The process of gathering and routing information, of guiding relationships and coaxing forth connections, strikes an educational note. Frances Hesselbein telling two team members to work things out between them, Nancy Badore devising a meeting "for them, not for me,"—both these women have something of the air of good teachers taking pains to help others learn, and knowing when to let students use what they have learned. But this teacher-like quality exhibited by the women in the diary studies does not seem unusual, since the teacher is most people's first model of female authority in the public realm.

As such, it informs ideas and assumptions about how women use power influence and create structures in order to lead.

THE STRATEGY
OF THE WEB

As we have seen, books such as *The Managerial Woman* attributed some measure of men's success in the workplace to what the authors saw as the male focus on "winning; on achieving a goal or reaching an objective." These goals or objectives were conceived of in very specific terms: bring in six new customers next month, make vice president within three years. By contrast, women were supposed to be hampered by a more diffuse, less goal-oriented notion of their careers: by tending to see their work "as personal growth, as self-fulfillment, as satisfaction, as making a contribution to others, as doing *what one wants to do.*"[5] The difference, then, came down to a question of *strategy:* men had a definite, objective plan for getting to where they wanted, while women, as a general rule, lacked such a plan.

And yet, when we consider the contrasting images of hierarchy and web, the question falls into a different focus. For what the authors of *The Managerial Woman* define as strategy is in fact the strategy of the hierarchy. It is preoccupied with targeting position, climbing the ladder, knocking out the competition, playing factions against each other, achieving an objective by manipulating the chain of command. Both its goals and methods assume the existence of a hierarchical structure.

This is surely how strategy is generally perceived, but it need not be the only way. The strategy of the web employs different methods in order to achieve different goals. Since the most desirable spot in the web is the center, the strategy of the web concentrates on drawing closer to that center by drawing others closer, and by strengthening the lines and orbs that knit the fabric together. Emphasizing interrelationships, working to tighten them, building up strength, knitting loose ends into the fabric, it is a strategy that honors the feminine principles of inclusion, connection, and what Carol Gilligan calls "being responsible in the world." And by emphasizing the *continual* drawing closer and strengthening of parts, it betrays the female's essential orientation toward *process,* her concern with the means used to achieve her ends.

The strategy of the web is less direct, less focused on specific goals, and so less driven by pure will than the strategy of the hierarchy. Thus it is appropriate to the diffuse and growth-centered notions of success that women have been criticized for holding. Proceeding by means of strengthening the fabric as well as defining a series of objectives, it works in a less linear fashion than hierarchical strategies.

British Prime Minister Margaret Thatcher, so often thought of as a woman who exemplifies male values, nevertheless gave perfect expression to this female sense of strategy when asked how she had attained her success. She replied that she had never spelled out specific goals for herself or aspired to a particular position, but had rather seized opportunities as they came and made the best of them.[6] Nancy Badore cited Thatcher's remarks when asked what her career objectives had been, and how she conceived her goals for the future. And Barbara Grogan echoed this theme: "I can't say where I'll be in five years; five years ago, I could never have foreseen where I am now. I don't draft five-year plans— I just do the best job I can, and trust that it will lead me to where I'm supposed to be next. I know that sounds sort of squishy, but it works."

Where I'm supposed to be next: clearly an element of trust is at work here; also a sense of fate, a conviction of destiny that is anything but passive. The strategy of the web is guided by opportunity, proceeds by the use of intuition, and is characterized by a patience that comes of waiting to see what comes next. It is the strategy used by the spider Charlotte in E. B. White's *Charlotte's Web.* When Charlotte is confronted by the need to save Wilbur, the barnyard pig facing slaughter, she does not devise a list of objectives in order to decide how to proceed. Instead of being "like men, who rush, rush, rush every minute," she relies on intuition and patience. "Charlotte knew from experience that if she waited long enough, a fly would come into her web; she felt sure that if she thought long enough about Wilbur's problem, an idea would come into her mind."[7] And the solution, when it came, required her to weave a web; after all, Charlotte "loved to weave, and she was an expert at it."

The image of weaving is one of the most ancient associated with the female domain; the archaic word for woman, *distaff*, also refers to a skein of flax, and to the staff on the loom that holds the unspun wool. In mythologies all over the world, female deities are depicted at the loom, knitting together the fabric of human life, spinning out the thread that links the events of the past with the potentialities—the unborn people and events—of the future. Thus the strategy of the web, of weaving, acknowledges the importance of what Frances Hesselbein called "the continuum," that sense that one is a part of what has gone before, and of what will follow.

For this reason, the spinning goddesses of Germanic and Greek myth were also the goddesses of fate. Their recognition and acceptance of destiny as the interweave of past and future, of chance and work, is the ultimate expression of the strategy of the web. And at the most profound level, this is what Barbara Grogan and Nancy Badore (and Margaret Thatcher) echo when they describe themselves as trusting that the opportunities which come their way will unlock their futures. Like the ancient female goddesses, they understand that the future cannot be reduced to a simple matter of objectives, nor achieved by the mere application of will.

PART II
The Diary Studies

CHAPTER THREE

The Heart of Belief Is Action

In doing the diary studies, what I sought above all was the feel of everyday details in the lives of the women with whom I spent time. I did not want to ask what they believed about what they were doing until I had watched them do it because, in the words of Don Burr, founder of People Express, "the heart of belief is action."

I did not choose the women for the diary studies randomly, but did many interviews first, casting around for subjects. I wanted to observe women who were strongly conscious of their management styles, and I wanted women who believed that gender *was* important, not only to who they were, but to how they did things. Each of the women I asked agreed quickly to be a subject, to let me come to her office and follow her around, taking notes on her every movement. Why would they agree to such scrutiny? I think the answer lies mainly in the fact that each is aware of herself as a role model, and makes use of her position in order to help other women. Appearing in print serves the end of fulfilling responsibility and fostering connection, so the women were content to let themselves be used as public examples, however inconvenient the process.

And it *was* inconvenient. The diary studies involved intense scrutiny, watching each subject from the moment she arrived at her office until the end of the working day, interrupting on occasion to ask what some acronym meant, or who that person was who stepped into the office. In an interview, the subject can censor out what she does not want to talk about, but in a diary study, there is no place to hide. During the day, the women were alone only in the bathroom.

The process took some getting used to. At the start of the day, I would describe myself as a fly on the wall, and request that my subject try to forget I was there as she went through her day. After an hour or so, something like this would happen, though I found that I had to keep reminding my subjects at intervals to ignore me. And of course my fly-on-the-wall invisibility existed as an ideal rather than something that could be achieved; like it or not, an observer always influences the observed to some degree. Then, of course, there was the fact that I had to interject questions, further destroying my efforts at invisibility.

As I recorded the details of my subjects' days, I paid particular attention to matters of scheduling, mail, phone calls, and interaction at meetings: the cues Mintzberg showed define the essence of a manager's style. I looked for patterns in how the women obtained and systematized information, made decisions, organized people and time, advised, explained, gave orders. In putting together these details, a picture emerged, or a rhythm: a flow, an ambiance, an atmosphere. I discovered that the pattern of a person's day is as distinct as his or her handwriting, giving clues to and revealing the human essence.

I also began to realize that the shape of a day, in all its detail and richness, is by its very nature a narrative. It has a beginning, an end, a form, an outline; things happen or they don't. Thus, as I wrote the studies, I did not have to risk the kind of distortion that, as a journalist, one can easily fall prey to in trying to turn an interview into "a story." The narratives take their natural form from the way the minutes of the day follow one another.

In Chapter 1, I addressed the reasons for writing the diary studies as narratives: I was looking for nuance as much as definition, and trying to put women's ways of leading into the context of greater social and economic change. But as I worked, I also began to realize that the differences in the way Mintzberg's and my diary studies are presented goes to the heart of the difference between how the men and women see themselves. His men function purely as managers, their identity seeming to exist in a vacuum, untouched by the details of their personal lives. By contrast, the women in the diary studies do not separate their personal selves from their workplace selves; they do not split being a mother off from being a manager, being an executive from being a friend. They conceive of their identities as integrated and whole, and draw strength from this integration, being always the same person even as they play the different roles that put various aspects of their characters into relief. As a result, I felt I had no choice but to render them as rounded human beings, painting pictures that were detailed not only in terms of events, but in terms of the living women who were my subjects.

CHAPTER FOUR

The Importance of Voice:

Frances Hesselbein,
Girl Scouts of the U.S.A.

P eter Drucker maintains that the leader of a well-run nonprofit organization is likely to be more skilled than the CEO of a profit-centered business, because the nonprofit manager must rely upon volunteers, who will simply devote their time elsewhere if the organization appears troubled. Thus the ability to motivate is absolutely paramount. Volunteers have no contractual relationship with the nonprofit organization they serve, but rather, in the phrase of Max De Pree, Chairman of Herman Miller, a *covenantal* one, which De Pree views as appropriate for our era. The voice of the covenantal leader must be strong but in no sense authoritarian; like Frances Hesselbein's, it must be the voice of welcome.

As National Executive Director of the Girl Scouts of the U.S.A., Frances Hesselbein holds the equivalent of the CEO's post in the largest nonprofit organization for girls and women in the non-Communist world. The Girl Scouts has more than three million members—nearly two and a half million girls, 750,000 adult volunteers, and a paid professional staff of 500. The national staff works out of a midtown Manhattan office building that is owned and fully occupied by the Girl Scouts. The yearly operating budget is $26 million.

Frances Hesselbein is the first chief executive from within the Girl Scouts' ranks. She began in the fifties as the temporary leader of a thirty-girl troop in her hometown of Johnstown, Pennsylvania, taking over reluctantly for a sick neighbor. "I had a son," she says, "so I wasn't much interested in the Girl Scouts." She promised she would keep the troop for a month, but ended up staying with it for eight years, loving "the excitement, the diversity, the intellectual challenge; also, I realized it was the kind of thing *I* would have loved as a girl." She describes her troop as "the laboratory" in which she formed her notions of what constituted good management. "I watched and helped the girls form committees, elect leaders, develop and meet objectives. Adults can learn so much by watching children, because children are starting the process from scratch. I always think of Chaucer's line about the Oxford scholar: 'Gladly did he learn and gladly teach.' That applies to my years with the girls."

While working with her troop, Frances Hesselbein was chosen president of the local council; soon afterward, she was asked by the national organization to train board members. It was then, during the sixties, that she began a serious study of management, reading "everything I could get my hands on." In 1970, she became executive director for her local council in Johnstown, her first paid staff post. In 1976, the board named her National Executive Director. By then she had moved to New York with her husband, who died in 1978.

At the time she assumed leadership, the Girl Scouts were re-examining how to meet the needs of a changing population of girls and a decline in the number of non-working mothers with time to serve as troop leaders. Frances Hesselbein moved quickly to reorganize, using the kind of marketing techniques and internal surveys she had learned about in her years of reading about management and training Girl Scout board members.

An internal marketing survey suggested that the 334 local councils would be better served if they were grouped according to common characteristics—such as urban or suburban, rather than geographical regions; the entire structure was reorganized in response. The corporate management team—another Hesselbein innovation—initiated "The Girl Scouts' Environmental Scanning System," an annual study of national statistics and trends covering everything from air pollution to unemployment; the idea was to anticipate large-scale demographic changes so that the organization could develop programs that would meet future needs. Two programs that evolved out of this were Safe Time, which keeps latchkey children occupied after school, and the Daisy Girl Scouts for five-year-olds, which included Head Start graduates; recently, a collaboration was begun between the Girl Scouts and Head Start.

In addition, she instituted a common planning and management system to unite the local councils. She developed a series of monographs that defined guidelines for financial reporting, equal employment, delivery systems, and nine other areas of concern; the management monograph series has since been adopted by public schools, not-for-profit organizations, and several major corporations. She revised the handbook and career pamphlets to reflect contemporary concerns, and emphasize the importance of math and science for girls. And she oversaw the building of the Edith Macy Conference Center in Westchester County, to provide volunteers and staff leaders with continuous professional training. The result has been what Peter Drucker describes as "the best-managed organization around. Tough, hardworking women can do anything."[1]

It is 8 A.M. on a July morning. Frances Hesselbein sits in her comfortable, airy green-and-peach office on the top floor of the Girl Scouts' building, dictating her first letter of the day. She is speaking into a machine; her voice is well modulated, measured and deliberate. From below comes the sound of rush hour traffic, but here on the fourteenth floor, rush and worry seem far away. Frances Hesselbein's calm voice sets the tone.

Her letter is to Dr. James Comer at the Yale Medical School. She received his new book, *Maggie's American Dream: The Life and Times of a Black American Family,* the story of Dr. Comer's mother, in yesterday's mail. The book now rests on the coffee table in front of the long green sofa in Frances Hesselbein's office. The table is stacked with the books she is currently reading and recommending.

She thanks Dr. Comer for the book, stops a moment to think, then says that his mother Maggie is "exactly the kind of woman who can provide a positive role model for our girls." She sips a little weak warm tea before dictating the closing paragraph, in which she promises Dr. Comer that she will pass his book around. She always drinks tea or hot water when she is using her voice to communicate—even if it's only to a dictating machine. "When you deliver a speech," she explains, "they usually provide a pitcher of ice water, but I found through experience that ice water makes my voice small and high. So I started asking for *hot* water or weak tea—it was an instinctual thing. Now I've found out from reading that my instincts were absolutely right! Cold closes vocal cords, warmth opens them up." She tells of reading an article about Jesse Jackson speaking after he had eaten a salty meal washed down with iced Coca-Colas, after which he didn't even sound like himself.

Finished with her letter to Dr. Comer, she dials the phone. It has a speaker attachment, but she doesn't use that impersonal device unless she's sharing the conversation with someone in her office. But now she is calling Michigan to offer sympathy to a young employee whose father died the previous week. "I sent flowers of course, but I felt that wasn't enough. It's so difficult to lose someone you love."

Frances Hesselbein knows this well. Just two nights before, several of her in-laws' relatives were killed instantly in a car crash. Strain from the tragedy shows slightly in her face; her usual calm is undisturbed, but her energy seems somewhat diminished. Still, she is keeping to her typical schedule: up at 6:00, a half hour of taped exercises that an instructor designed just for her, a walk from her apartment to her midtown office— "exactly twenty-two minutes." But because of the accident, she has canceled the vacation she had scheduled for next week, and this means that today's load of work will be lighter than usual. "More in keeping with what I feel I can handle at such a sad time."

After her call to Michigan, she steps out from behind her desk. Frances Hesselbein is a short woman with perfect posture; she doesn't reveal her age. She moves with vigor and her beautiful clear skin makes her seem almost ageless. Her dark hair, swept back in a kind of pageboy, is neatly styled, her nails manicured; she has an old-fashioned quality of perfect grooming. Today she is dressed in a hot pink silk suit, black linen blouse, black stockings, expensive black shoes, understated gold jewelry, and a Girl Scout pin. She is a woman who favors Hermès scarves and bags; her style is elegant, ladylike, and timeless.

She steps into the hall outside her office, where her three secretaries work. She asks the one who is not on the phone to call a limousine to take Ann Millhouse, the chief commissioner of the Girl Guides in Australia, to the airport. Mrs. Millhouse has been in New York for a few days, studying some of the management techniques that Frances Hesselbein has put in place at the Girl Scouts. Mrs. Millhouse and her husband are staying in the small hotel around the corner from the Girl Scouts' midtown building, and Frances Hesselbein has promised to order them a car. "And I will stop by to see them off personally," she tells the secretary. "Please remind me if I haven't left the office by nine-thirty."

It is now 8:20. One of the secretaries buzzes Frances Hesselbein to ask if she has time to meet briefly with Florence Corsello, the controller and financial director of the Girl Scouts, and a member of the corporate management team. Frances Hesselbein says she would be glad to see her, and a few minutes later Florence Corsello enters her office; she is a young woman and wears a conservative accountant's suit. Frances Hesselbein welcomes her warmly and leads her to an upholstered chair, then sits down opposite her on the sofa.

From the small adjoining room that serves as a lavatory, kitchen, and extra closet, one of Frances Hesselbein's secretaries serves tea in china cups. The atmosphere in the comfortable room piled with books is relaxed. Florence Corsello follows what seems to be the common practice of those who work closely with Frances Hesselbein of addressing her as Frances, but referring to her as Mrs. Hesselbein when speaking to others.

They discuss the Australian leader's visit briefly, agreeing that it was a great success, with plenty of information exchanged on both sides. "She was surprised by the variety of girls we are able to reach out to," says Frances Hesselbein. During her tenure, minority membership in the Girl Scouts has tripled.

She tells Florence Corsello about the Australian leader's husband, a criminal court judge, and describes the dinners they all had together over the weekend. "It was a good time, though of course difficult under the circumstances." Avoiding any awkwardness, she immediately brings up her family tragedy. "I don't want people to have to guess what is going on," she explained. "The funeral will be small and very private. And I have canceled my vacation in England next week."

Florence Corsello murmurs her regrets.

"This teaches us one thing," says Frances Hesselbein. "We never know what is going to happen, so we must cherish every moment."

She asks Florence Corsello about the contracts on a major study that the Girl Scouts are undertaking with Dr. Robert Coles of Harvard and the Lou Harris organization on the beliefs and moral values of young people today. Its purpose is to provide the Girl Scouts with data about how girls are thinking, so that programs addressing their concerns can be developed.

"This is something we really have to stay on top of." Frances Hesselbein stirs her tea. "Could you make a couple of calls today?"

"I'll do it before the meeting," says Florence Corsello, referring to the monthly corporate management team meeting, which is scheduled for today at noon.

They discuss the meeting's agenda, then Frances Hesselbein mentions how pleased she is with the hotel accounting system recently installed in the Girl Scouts' new Edith Macy Conference Center in Westchester County. "You did a wonderful, very professional job with it. I'm so pleased!" They discuss some tapes Peter Drucker made recently on effective management. Frances Hesselbein urges Florence to listen to them. "They're great for stirring up your thinking."

Then she picks up *Maggie's American Dream* from the coffee table, and suggests that Florence read the book. She tells her a few anecdotes from what she has already read. "And I can't wait to read more! I wrote Dr. Comer to thank him this morning."

Florence observes that Frances Hesselbein is scrupulous about answering mail immediately—and always holds her managers to her own high standard. Frances Hesselbein smiles and explains that every piece of mail addressed to the Girl Scouts must be answered within three days. She says her dictating machine enables her to do this. "I have one here, and I also have one at home. It's the only way I can keep on top of things."

At 9:10 Florence Corsello leaves the office. Frances Hesselbein has spent nearly half an hour with her. Only two direct pieces of business have been discussed: the contracts on the study of young people's values, and the agenda for the management team meeting. Altogether, these items took about ten minutes. The rest of the time was spent in more informal conversation, though everything said related in some way to the Girl Scouts.

Most notable about the meeting was its relaxed, unhurried pace. There was no sense that outside concerns might be pressing. "I am very deliberate about trying to create a calm atmosphere," says Frances Hesselbein. "I do this even at times when I feel far from relaxed inside. Or sad or upset about something, as now. It's a question of discipline and commitment, of what you've decided is most important. I've trained myself to take time with people, to really listen to what they say, because I believe that *they* are the important part of my job. Some managers are always worrying about paperwork, or what they have to do next. But you can wedge your paperwork in anytime. I try not to give people the feeling I'm rushed. For example, I never look at my watch if I'm talking with someone. I think that's such an insulting gesture! It suggests you're trying to gauge whether you think what they're saying is worth your time. Rushing is no way to bring out what's best in people, and I'm always looking for the best. That's what's ultimately behind my determination to take my time."

As important as her calm, welcoming tone, Frances Hesselbein believes, is the language she uses: taken together, tone and words create the voice, and the voice is the outer manifestation of the speaker's essence. For Frances Hesselbein, leadership is really a question of voice, of representing her essence in the strongest possible way. "I feel passionately about how I express myself. Language is the greatest motivating force. You can phrase something positively and inspire people to do their best, or negatively and make them feel worried, uncertain, and self-conscious. You can talk at a fast pace"—here she speeds up her own speech for a moment—"and people will get nervous, feel afraid to bring up extraneous thoughts. But those are the very thoughts that might be most important! They might represent that person's best thinking. If you're rushed, you're simply not going to get at that extra level of thinking. Marshall Goldsmith (a speaker and writer on leadership) talks about the importance of making people feel they're bringing something of value to your organization. You do this by communicating *respect* in the way you use your voice."

She digs out a popular management book from the pile on the coffee table, opens it and shakes her head in disgust. "The *language* in this—I can truthfully say it's everything we try to avoid!" She puts on a gruff, swaggering tone. " 'Here's the battle plan!' " She shudders. "I wouldn't want to talk like that even if it were effective, which I don't believe it is."

Another kind of language she tries to avoid is business jargon. "You won't hear us talking here about segments or products. One out of four girls between six and eight in the U.S. is a Brownie, but we don't use that statistic to talk about a 'one-in-four market share.' And we don't 'target' groups. A six-year-old child is not a target! We use language that reflects human ways of thinking about people. And I never permit anyone to refer to our organization as a big business, just because we have an operating budget of twenty-six million dollars. We are a well-managed enterprise that has as its purpose changed lives, so we use language that presents a message of caring. And I try—even on a day like today, when I'm not feeling my best—to use my own voice in a way that shows caring, respect, appreciation, and patience. Your voice, your language, help determine your *culture*. And part of how a corporate culture is defined is how the people who work for an organization use language."

From 9:10 to 9:30 Frances Hesselbein is at her desk, placing calls to the five guest speakers she has invited to participate in the Girl Scouts' upcoming meeting of executive directors—"my counterparts on the local level." The meeting is scheduled for mid-September in St. Louis. Frances Hesselbein always invites speakers to this gathering, usually someone who can address a "nuts-and-bolts kind of issue—fund-raising, or something like that." But this year, she wants to turn the three-day gathering into a "rare and wonderful intellectual adventure" by inviting well-known speakers to address the conferees on such issues as trends, demographics, leadership, and ethics—"in order to help people look at what we're doing from the really big perspective of social change."

She plans to send each of the directors who will be attending the St. Louis meeting a study packet containing the most recent books and magazine articles by each speaker. Now she is arranging for the material to be sent, making the follow-up calls herself. As she talks with the speakers' representatives or publishers, she is careful to mention what she has been doing to promote their work. Talking with one of Peter Drucker's assistants, she tells him that the head of the Australian Girl Guides has purchased a complete set of his new management tapes, and she reports on colleagues who have ordered tapes through her in bulk.

Between calls, she dictates a letter that will be sent to each of the speakers. "This is what I mean by being able to wedge in paperwork anytime." Using both phone and dictating machine, she keeps her voice calm and deliberately paced, which seems to help keep her on an even keel.

At 9:30 she picks up a chit from her secretary to pay the airport limousine, then steps outside the building into Manhattan's traffic. She walks around the block to the hotel where the head of the Australian Girl Guides and her husband have been staying, and waits for them in the lobby. When the car arrives, she pays the driver, then returns to find her guests stepping off the elevator; she picks up one of their suitcases and helps them to the car—purely a polite gesture, since two bellboys are in attendance. She and the Australian leader discuss the fine days they have spent together, then promise to keep in touch by sending one another books and letters.

Back in the office by 10:00, Frances Hesselbein jots a handwritten memo to the head of the Girl Scouts' human resources department, asking him to put the Australian Girl Guides' chief commissioner on her permanent mailing list. "I usually do handwritten notes to my staff people," she explains. Then she writes four more memos, working from the reminder list she makes up every night at home just before she goes to bed. There are fifteen entries on it, mostly names of people to write or call.

Several calls come in from the guest speakers who will be at the St. Louis meeting in September; they are returning Frances Hesselbein's earlier calls. She is in the process of putting together study packets of their most recent work, which she will mail to all the conferees well in advance of the meeting. "That way, they'll really be prepared for the discussions." The packet includes *On Becoming a Leader* by Warren Bennis, *The New Realities* by Peter Drucker, *A Study in Excellence: Management in the Non-Profit Human Services* by Marshall Goldsmith, Michael Josephson's *Ethics* magazine, and a recent keynote speech to the National Urban League's annual conference by John Jacob.

She spends ten minutes making changes in the large desk calendar she keeps. She also has a calendar at home, and a third for traveling; in addition, her three secretaries have a calendar. Updating and coordinating them all is a constant task, though not one that consumes much time—like paperwork, it is something that Frances Hesselbein believes can be "wedged in."

Now, as soon as she has finished updating her desk calendar, she calls for one of her secretaries so that she can update the secretarial calendar as well. "It's an ongoing process," Frances Hesselbein explains. "Also, the secretaries can come into my office and make changes on my calendar here. The important thing is not who does what, but making sure that we all keep together."

At 10:20 another secretary enters with a folder marked with the day's date; it contains about twelve pieces of mail. "They give it to me in manageable packets like this, not in great big masses." Each piece has been marked with two stamps: one shows the date it was received, the other has space for a file number and the initials of whoever will answer it. This system helps Frances Hesselbein to make sure that every letter received by her office is answered within the requisite three days.

She reads the first letter. The director of a technical education association is writing to congratulate the Girl Scouts on their work in encouraging young girls to study math and science. Frances Hesselbein dictates a reply immediately. "Of course, this is the kind of letter I respond to *personally*. Any positive comment deserves my recognition." She believes it is very important not to reserve priority responses for mail that makes specific requests or concerns arrangements. "Mail that essentially just keeps one in touch, or helps build bridges and connections between people, is really the most important kind of all."

There are newsclippings as well as mail in the file. She hands one clip to the secretary. "Please put this in the fat file," she advises, referring to the many letters of complaint the Girl Scouts have begun to receive concerning the use of tropical oils in their cookies.

It is 10:40. Another secretary brings in a stack of periodicals. Frances Hesselbein carries them to the long green sofa. She scans an article in *The Non-Profit Times* and, finding a reference to the Girl Scouts, underlines it and attaches a Post-it tab to the page. She does this with all books and magazines when she finds a mention of the organization, and then makes a point of showing them around—to staff, or to whoever comes into her office.

She scans *Ethics* magazine, put out by the Josephson Ethics Institute, of which she is a board member; she places it on the coffee table with her stack of books. She is as scrupulous about updating the reading matter on this table as she is about keeping her calendars in sync; she uses the pile of books and magazines to make her current recommendations. Recommending books is an important part of her job, she believes; "a way of putting people you work with in touch with new ideas." As I take notes, she digs out a copy of Bill Moyers' *A World of Ideas*, adapted from his PBS interview series. "I strongly recommend this. You can read it in little chunks.

So stimulating! And it's a perfect gift for people in the hospital."

She scans a copy of *Management Review*, taking time to read an interview with Nehama Jacobs, who with Sarah Hardesty wrote *Success and Betrayal: The Crisis of Women in Corporate America*, a book she greatly admires. She is excited by the article's premise that even companies that don't particularly want to hire and promote women or develop day-care policies will have to do so in years ahead. "Anything I read, I ask myself, how does this apply to the Girl Scouts? What are the implications for the future of girls? When you look at it like that—really try to take in the whole picture—you realize that *everything* has some application."

She spends a full half hour scanning the periodicals, interrupted by four brief telephone calls. "When I travel a lot, as I have been doing lately, I always schedule a morning like this to take care of details, and be really thorough in dealing with publications. It's important to keep some time free of scheduled meetings; it's one of the things I do to pace myself. And not only does unscheduled time enable me to keep up with what's going on, but puttering around like this also gives me a chance to *think*."

In an earlier interview, when I asked Frances Hesselbein about the source of the energy that permits her to keep going from 6:00 each morning until after 10:00 most nights, Bonnie McEwan, the Girl Scouts' media services director, mentioned her boss's skill at scheduling in bits of free time throughout the day, using odd moments not to cram in extra chores but to really relax. Bonnie McEwan noted how, when traveling for a speaking engagement, Frances Hesselbein would usually arrange to arrive the night before; if she was going to do a videotaped appearance, she would even schedule in a whole extra day after traveling to rest and take care of little details. Frances Hesselbein laughed in response. "Oh, that's just vanity! One advantage to being a woman is that you're always aware if there are going to be bags under your eyes, so you try to schedule in rest in order to deal with that problem."

At 11:10 she asks a secretary to order her a BLT sandwich for the noon meeting of corporate management staff. This is a monthly meeting; she usually tries to keep her lunch hour free for reading and conserving energy for the rest of the day. Then she takes an elevator to the twelfth floor, where Bonnie McEwan meets her. Together they go to the small video editing room where Frances Hesselbein is scheduled to view the rough cut of a television spot recently done pro bono for the Girl Scouts by a large advertising agency. The spot has an MTV format and the mind-numbing pulse of synthetic percussion; nothing could be more unlike Frances Hesselbein's dignified style.

"This is not meant to appeal to adults," she says. "It's aimed at young girls, who are used to watching this sort of thing. But I think it's very good. Really excellent!" She asks to see the tape of last months' investiture at the White House of Barbara Bush as honorary national president. When the screening is over, she compliments the young editor on her work.

At 11:30 she is back in her office, consulting her yellow-pad reminder list. She calls the author of a newly published book on affirmative action to tell him that she used his book at a recent seminar. "I always think it's nice to try to give an author some feedback on his work," she explains. Next, she dictates a memo to her staff about possible conflicts over vacation time during a conference to be held over the Labor Day weekend.

The three secretaries are constantly in and out of her office. I ask if there is a division of labor among them; does each handle a different kind of work? "Mrs. Hesselbein would like there to be," says Marguerite Hanor, referring to her boss in the formal way that all employees do, unless speaking to her directly. Marguerite Hanor has the title of Special Assistant for Corporate Administration and, unlike the two other secretaries, works from a private office, but despite this she makes no claim of privilege. "We all do everything, share the work—there's no room around here for a star, for someone to think she's above the others. You're expected to pitch in on whatever needs doing. Nothing is beneath your dignity. But on the other hand, nothing is beyond your reach."

Frances Hesselbein agrees. "They use the team approach. By that I mean they don't divide the jobs—say, one would do the calendar and the other would type up what I record on the Dictaphone. I used to try to get them to do that, feeling it would be easier for me. But they all agreed that their system worked most efficiently for them, so I just had to live with their team approach to management."

Given the number of calls that come through the office, how do the secretaries know who to put through? Marguerite Hanor explains, "There are about twenty people we know Mrs. Hesselbein will always talk to; and of course she tells us if there's anyone special she's expecting to hear from on a given day. Also, because we're constantly in touch with her calendar, we can handle a lot of calls ourselves—we just use our judgment, and she *never* second-guesses us. The thing is, she's very accessible by phone. She's not one to hide in her office, or use other people to help her hide." Marguerite Hanor adds that the office runs smoothly because "Mrs. Hesselbein is absolutely unflappable. She is *the* most even-tempered person I've ever known. And that sets the tone around here. We're free to concentrate on getting things done, instead of worrying about who's supposed to do what, who'll get the credit, or whose territory is being invaded. Or if the boss is going to let us have it for some mistake."

At 11:50 Frances Hesselbein goes into the small room adjoining her office to freshen herself for the management team meeting; she is a woman who puts on fresh lipstick before doing a telephone interview. At exactly noon she leaves for the eleventh-floor conference center, a serene but rather institutional-looking room done in muted neutral shades. On the far wall hang pictures of every national president beginning with Juliette Low, founder of the American Girl Scouts. The picture gallery provides a fascinating study in changing styles of female dignity, bringing to mind the succession of Betty Crocker images that General Mills has featured throughout the years.

Six of the seven senior staff members are gathered; the other is on vacation. Everyone sits when he or she is ready. The atmosphere is easy and informal. The staff members here comprise the inner circle of the management web that Frances Hesselbein composed for me with cutlery at the Cosmopolitan Club; they report to her directly. The circular management structure she has put in effect is affectionately referred to around Girl Scout Headquarters as "the bubble chart," though as previously mentioned, Peter Drucker calls it "The Girl Scouts' Wheel of Fortune."

Everyone has brought their own lunch. Frances Hesselbein's BLT, ordered by a secretary, awaits her at the head of the large oval table. At every place is a one-page printed agenda for the day's meeting. Everyone has brought notebooks, pads, and pens. Frances Hesselbein opens her folder, which contains a yellow legal pad on which she makes notes and doodles during the course of the meeting.

She opens the meeting by recounting the time she has

just spent with "our Australian visitor." She describes
problems faced by the Girl Guides in Australia. There
are the difficult legal questions, also faced by groups like
the Girl Scouts here, about the viability of organizations
that define themselves as serving a single sex. "They're
under attack there, the same as here. All in the name
of promoting coeducation." She pauses and shakes her
head. "But it's important for all of us to be aware of
developments like this in other countries. It helps us get
an idea of general world trends."

A discussion follows, loose and informal, with lots of
questions about the visit. Australia becomes a general
topic. Everyone eats sandwiches and passes around the
Girl Scout cookies and peanut brittle that are a part of
every gathering. After a half hour, when the meal is
finished, Frances Hesselbein pours a cup of tea and puts
on lipstick, a signal that the scheduled part of the meeting is about to begin.

"I'll open by sharing with you something of my last
conversation with Betty Pilsbury," she says, referring to
the Girl Scouts' president, a volunteer elected by the
board of directors. Betty Pilsbury is concerned about a
controversy that has developed regarding the Girl Scouts'
sale of 14,000 wilderness acres in Wyoming. Frances
Hesselbein asks Florence Corsello, the controller, to
keep the president up-to-date on the matter, sending her
all memos and correspondence. She says that a demonstration against the sale of the land has been planned
by a group for the following day. "They are supposed

to be here, in front of our building, at ten o'clock. In case they do show up, I want everyone to know our policy: we will invite them in to discuss the matter, *and* we will serve them tea." She pauses. "No, in July, we'd better make that iced drinks. And of course, Girl Scout cookies." She asks two staff members to please "take charge of making sure we treat our demonstrators well."

Several people seem flustered at the notion of a demonstration, but Frances Hesselbein remains in control, her voice never losing its warm, calm tone. Leading the meeting, she speaks very slowly, again as if she had all the time in the world. But that relaxation is all in the sound of her voice; the tempo, once the first half hour of general discussion has been gotten out of the way, moves decisively along.

It is now 12:50. Next on the agenda is a membership update by Assistant National Director Mary Rose Main. "Mary Rose, why don't you give us the sad news on membership?" says Frances Hesselbein in an ironic tone.

Mary Rose Main laughs as she passes around a photocopy of membership figures for the last month. "You'll see that once again we've exceeded our highest projections." There is some discussion of which regions have shown stronger growth than others, and an examination of possible reasons for this.

Then Frances Hesselbein asks John Sokolowski, the only male member present, to give his monthly report on the sales of various Girl Scout items—guidebooks, uniforms, and cookies. As he lists the figures, she leans forward intently while other staff members question him in an informal way. Occasionally, she interjects a compliment on someone's observation; she appears always to be looking for ways to praise.

A conflict arises over the printing of a council service publication; certain departments have not filled out their forms correctly. While others discuss which departments have been lax, Frances Hesselbein mostly listens, asking an occasional question: "Any suggestions on how we can get that done?" She never tries to arbitrate the dispute that has arisen, or assert authority in any direct way; she listens and watches, doodling on her pad. Later she will explain, "I *never* adjudicate with senior staff. I expect them to work problems out among themselves. If I get involved, then every time a dispute arises, people will feel as if they have to know what *I* think. They won't take responsibility among themselves." She points out that such an approach cuts back on the kind of jockeying for support that can turn staff meetings into quests for political approval.

The dispute over printing does not resolve itself. Sensing that the discussion is taking too much time, Frances Hesselbein tells the two principals to "please work together on this, and report back to me when you've come to an agreement." She adds that it is time to move on to the next item on the agenda, but suggests that everyone first take a ten-minute break to stretch.

It is 1:15. Frances Hesselbein goes briefly to her office to check her calls. When she returns, she again lets the meeting come spontaneously to order. After five minutes of informal talking, she refers to the agenda. "Now, I'd like some feedback on those Drucker tapes I handed out last time." She frequently gives such homework assignments to members of her senior staff as a way to keep them "stretching and growing."

The Drucker tapes—to which she has referred at various moments during the day—are a set of audiocassettes that feature a roundtable discussion on management; Peter Drucker is the moderator, and Frances Hesselbein is one of the participants. She is eager that the tapes get plenty of airing because she thinks they are both innovative and important, and because she wants her staff to keep abreast of new ideas that relate to management. "Now, while the reviews are coming out," she says, "we ought to be thinking up innovative ways to sell the tapes. Maybe get small groups together to listen and discuss them? I'd like to get everyone's best thinking on this."

She asks for memos from everyone at the table on the subject, then she moves on to give a brief status report on funding sources for the study on young people's values that the Girl Scouts is undertaking with Harvard. A staff member asks when they can start telling the local councils about the project. "The minute we have the contracts signed. We must be absolutely *sure* that the councils are informed before the news releases go out. We can't have anyone feeling left out on this one."

Next on the agenda is Mary Rose Main's discussion of the corporate management team retreat, which was held the previous month at a Connecticut inn. The purpose was for senior management to spend intensive time identifying the most important objectives for the next fiscal year, which will begin in October. From the larger Tactical Planning Schedule, devised eighteen months before, nineteen priorities have been identified. A three-page summary of these points is now handed around the table.

Everyone spends a few minutes reading it. "Now," says Frances Hesselbein, "we all know how important this memo is. It gives us the big picture of what direction we need to be going in, cutting away all the small tasks so we don't get lost in the day-to-day. It looks good to me, but we need to *think* about it. Is this really meaningful? Is it something you'd take to bed with you?"

A discussion follows, which Frances Hesselbein leads by asking questions. But as answers are volunteered, she does not seem satisfied. Instead, she continues to ask more questions, to probe for deeper thoughts. "Is there anything else we can do on this? What might be some other options?" Using this brainstorming approach, she continually broadens the discussion, always focusing on the larger issues. When someone suggests that a twentieth point be added about the Girl Scouts' commitment to equal access, Frances Hesselbein widens this to a more general discussion of the Supreme Court's recent rulings on civil rights. "We need to think carefully about *all* the Supreme Court decisions in terms of how they relate to what we're doing. They're a source of real change in this country, and we need to follow them closely. For example, making *this* point should lead us to ask ourselves what our commitment to equal access means in an era when that priority is not mandated by the court. How does it strengthen our attitude? What are the dangers?"

Mary Rose Main hands out copies of the full Tactical Planning Schedule for 1990—a thick white notebook with the full year's plans. The nineteen-point memo was a distillation of the tactical schedule for the previous year. These tactical schedules are made up each year by the management staff; they lay out the operational plan for achieving the overall objectives that have been set and defined by the board in the six-year Strategic Plan. The strategic and the tactical plans—together with the yearly performance appraisals done by both management staff and the board—comprise the overall corporate planning system that Frances Hesselbein instituted when she assumed directorship.

The Tactical Plan in its thick white notebook defines every objective for the coming year in quantifiable terms: for example, a 2 percent increase in membership; a 4 percent increase in minority Girl Scouts; the widening of opportunities for older girls west of the Mississippi. These objectives are then broken down into detailed "action steps," which are assigned to different management groups. Projects are developed to achieve specific objectives; if a conference is called for, the details are spelled out—where it will be held, the theme, and who will produce the resources. The entire program is then costed out and presented as the yearly budget for the board's approval. Every one of the 500 staff members contributes to the Tactical Plan, which records the number of working hours allotted to achieve each goal. "Everything interlocks with each other," explains Mary Rose Main. "The smaller tasks with the larger, the smaller units performing each task with the larger units." In addition, the Tactical Plan is used at the end of the year to evaluate individual performance, so that these may be judged concretely in terms of goals met.

Everyone takes about ten minutes to glance through the heavy notebook. Then Frances Hesselbein suggests another break. It is just after 2:00. When everyone returns, another conflict arises. Mary Rose Main mentions her recent discussion with the head of a foundation that helps homeless families; the group will be holding a series of yard sales in various cities around the United States, and she wonders if there is any way for the Girl Scouts to become involved. Dori Parker, another member of the team, objects: this could conflict with guidelines that prohibit any fund-raising in the organization. Frances Hesselbein does not intervene during the discussion, but listens as it takes its course. Finally, after ten fruitless minutes, she charges the two disagreeing staff members to come to a decision on the matter between themselves, and then report back to her with their agreement.

The final item on the agenda is marked "other" in order to accommodate free discussion. Frances Hesselbein begins by outlining the schedule for the big St. Louis meeting in September, advising everyone to arrive on the preceding night in order to allow "plenty of time to relax and get organized." She talks about the study packet she will be sending to all conferees. "Isn't it wonderful? We're going to be sending out all these new books. But we'll only send them a few at a time, or else people will feel overwhelmed and not bother to read them."

As the meeting draws to a close, she begins recommending other books. She mentions *Maggie's American Dream.* "I can't wait to get home and read more of it tonight!" She asks if everyone has received the copies she sent out of the Yale commencement address by Benno Schmidt. "It's *very* powerful. I'm so pleased to see something being written nowadays with such great historical perspective!"

She closes the meeting by telling everyone of her changed vacation plans, and mentioning all the kind remarks she has received about her relatives who just died. She then repeats what she said this morning, when Florence Corsello was in her office. "All we can learn from something like this is to cherish every moment. Life is very, very precious."

As the group breaks up, Frances Hesselbein says she would like to schedule a meeting the following week with the expanded management team—the second and third tiers of the circle—which comprises about fifty staff people. There is a brief discussion of a time for the meeting, then everyone returns to his or her office. The meeting has lasted a full three hours, not unusual for this monthly gathering. The day, however, is unusual for Frances Hesselbein, in that this is her only scheduled meeting. She usually spends about 40 percent of her week in meetings in and outside the office.

Back in her office at just after 3:00, she picks up two new folders of mail that have come in, and glances through about fifteen items. "On a day like today, when I don't have many meetings, I use my time in my office to connect with the outside world—that's what mail is, a link to the world. Drucker describes the CEO as a *hinge* that connects the organization to its board of directors, and to the whole world beyond. So to be a good hinge, you've got to keep your outside connections strong."

She uses the dictating machine to do six more letters, then at 3:30 she makes two last phone calls to coordinate final materials for the study packet she is putting together for the local executive directors. A secretary brings in a Mailgram about a Girl Scout ceremony that President Bush will be hosting. Frances Hesselbein writes out an immediate response.

At 4:00 she carries a stack of magazines that came in during the week to the long green sofa in her office.

Since she didn't have time to read over lunch, she will do it now. She believes that keeping up with reading is one of the most important aspects of how she manages, and she is constantly circulating and recommending books to colleagues and subordinates. "I read about three hours a day," she says. "I'm like a dachshund—they're eager eaters. In order to make time for all that reading, I have to schedule it all in."

What does she read? "To start with, all the good management books. I try to take a look at everything that comes out. And of course all the relevant magazines, and the New York *Times* and other papers—though I usually don't get around to those until after ten at night. I also read a lot of history and biography, especially about women. And I'm partial to anything that relates to England—my family background is English. I pick up a good paperback mystery sometimes, especially if I have a long plane trip. Traveling is a great time for reading. At home, I often read cookbooks. I feel the need to because I don't have time to cook anymore, and cooking is something I always enjoyed. Now I cook only on Thanksgiving and Christmas, when I make my grandmother's ritual meal. It has to be *exactly* the same each year, down to the bowl the cranberries are served in."

As she reads, she underlines passages and attaches Post-it tabs to pages she wants to mark. This enables her to find exact quotes very quickly. Now, as she gives *Management Review* a more thorough reading, I glance through the books on her coffee table—her current

101

books, the ones she keeps out for referral and recommendations. In addition to *Maggie's American Dream*
and Bill Moyers' *World of Ideas,* they are *The Executive
Odyssey* by Frederick Harmon; *The Moral Life of Children* by Robert Coles; a picture book of Johnstown,
Pennsylvania; several paperback guides to teaching children about different cultures; and a thick book called
*Making a Leadership Change: How Organizations and
Leaders Can Handle Leadership Transitions Successfully*
by Thomas North Gilmore.

This last tome has become a kind of Bible for Frances
Hesselbein during this past year, for in 1990 she plans
to leave her position after a thirteen-and-a-half-year tenure—unusually long for a national executive director in
this organization. She will devote herself to lecturing,
writing, and serving on various boards in the years
ahead, but for now, she is studying this book on transition, for she is convinced that one's skill as a manager
is best rated "not by how smoothly things run while
you're there, but how well they go after you have left."
Many lines in the book, and whole paragraphs, have
been blocked out in yellow marker, and there are handwritten notes in the margins. Next to one sentence, in
which the author discusses the case of "a new leader
with little information on existing staff," Frances Hesselbein has written in a neat but strong handwriting that
seems the visual counterpart of her voice: *"Our* new
leader will have plenty!"

She spends a full forty-five minutes reading. At 4:45

she announces her intention of going home. "I am almost always here until six, but now I am going home and go right to bed. You have to do that sometimes, you know, in order to catch up on your sleep. Conserving energy is very important. And you know my philosophy of scheduling in breaks." With her usual calm deliberation, she clears her desk, then leaves to take a bus back to the apartment tower where she lives alone on a high floor. She says that, having grown up in the mountains of western Pennsylvania, she has an almost physical need for a view: "That's what keeps me going, gives me my inspiration." Her view from her apartment is of the East River and Queens beyond, but she likes to pretend to herself that it is of Maui. "I like to pretend I have that far a view. Seeing far is what gives me energy, so I like to look out on my Hawaiian mountain."

CHAPTER FIVE

The Structure of Spontaneity:

Barbara Grogan,
Western Industrial Contractors

B arbara Grogan's schedule is highly demanding and carefully planned; with a small company that has a single secretary and a heavy load of out-of-office events, she keeps her own calendar. This she organizes down to the minute in a highly conscious fashion, declaring that "minutes are bits of yourself that you give away." Despite the pace and the need for structure, Barbara Grogan uses her organizational skills to free rather than to drive herself. She knows exactly how much time she must spend in a given place, so once she is there, she is completely *there*. She is a woman who lives intensely in the present, wresting all she can from each moment, responding to whatever happens spontaneously. But she can live with this vivid sense of enjoyment and unusual responsiveness only because she has planned her every move in advance. When she is making that move, she doesn't have to think about what she will be doing next. It's the essence of organization, and it's profoundly liberating.

Barbara Grogan, forty-three years old, is founder and president of Western Industrial Contractors, a $6 million millwrighting firm in Denver, Colorado. She started the company with $50,000 and an old pickup truck in 1982, during the darkest days of Denver's oil-business recession. At that time, construction companies were losing their business base; in the shakeout that followed, many did not survive. But Barbara Grogan, one of less than a dozen women among the nearly 5,000 millwrighting contractors nationwide, has not only survived but flourished, attracting national clients such as AT&T, Anheuser-Busch, the Manville Corporation, United Airlines, and IBM. In 1986 Barbara Grogan added a consulting division to provide clients with estimating, scheduling, and cost-control services in all phases of the construction business. The consulting company recently won a $1 million contract to do the scheduling for Denver's new international airport.

Millwrighting is a highly specialized and complex business that involves the moving and installation of industrial equipment. Barbara Grogan's company has moved a pipe manufacturing plant from Florida to Malaysia, installed the world's largest underground baggage sorting system at United's beautiful new O'Hare terminal, hung a four-story theater screen, erected an automated warehouse from thousands of stacked metal shelves, and relocated $7 million flight simulators used to train airline pilots. Such jobs require mammoth equipment—twenty-story cranes, twenty-four-wheel trucks— and also, paradoxically, precision. The installation of a mylar press at an IBM plant, for example, permitted only one ten thousandth of an inch in error.

Barbara Grogan never intended to get into business for herself at all. "I had been raised as a Cinderella," she explains. "I never had any idea of supporting myself." After graduating from the University of Colorado with a psychology degree, she worked for a while in the research department of Mountain Bell, then got married at the age of twenty-three. Her husband ran a truck and crane leasing company, and although she helped him in the office during a nine-month period, she never imagined herself in any phase of the business; she concentrated on being a wife and mother. "When people asked me how long I'd been married, I used to say, 'Since I was two,' since that's when I began thinking that my major role in life would be as somebody's wife and mother."

Then, when she was thirty-five, she and her husband divorced and she was left with two children. "I was devastated. Plus, I was faced with the prospect of having to earn a living. It was a matter of having to put food on the table." Her self-esteem was so low from the divorce that she felt sure no one would hire her; starting a business seemed the only alternative. She settled on the idea of becoming a contractor, because "as a contractor you don't need to own your own equipment. You lease everything and hire on a project basis. Contracting is very labor-intensive, so it's the perfect business for someone with very little money and less potential for raising any."

Barbara Grogan has succeeded in a tough market at a bad time because of her company's commitment to excellence, attentive service, and a policy of nurturing client relationships with the long term in mind. She is determined that Western Industrial Contractors "never takes advantage of a client in a bad position." For example, when a 6 A.M. explosion at the client's cement factory knocked a kiln out of operation, Barbara Grogan got a supervisor and eleven millwrights on the site by 9 A.M. They worked in round-the-clock shifts for four days, yet she charged the regular fees—unusual in the business. "We don't look at the bottom line to see how much money we can make on a job," she explains. "Our goal is to keep our clients coming back for more."

This focus on the long term is also apparent in how Barbara Grogan handles the highly visible leadership role she has begun to assume in Denver. Working from her position on the board of directors of the Greater Denver Chamber of Commerce, she has become an advocate for small business, which she sees as the key to a healthy and broad-based recovery for the region. The governor recently appointed her to head his Small Business Advisory Council, which provides her with a platform in the public sector. As her business continues to grow, she is spending more and more time outside the office.

It is 7:00 on a clear bright Denver morning, and Barbara Grogan is driving her big Dodge van along the almost deserted downtown street. She drives slowly, at a deliberate pace, taking time to look out the window at the blaze of snow-covered mountains rising to meet the clouds in the west. On the dashboard above her cellular phone is a printed placard that reads, "I am powerful, beautiful, creative, and I can handle it!" The message— part mantra, part script, part reminder—was given her by a friend to help her through tough times.

She parks in a downtown lot across from the Greater Denver Chamber of Commerce and crosses the street. She is a lively, attractive woman, and on this May morning she wears a tailored black-and-white blazer, black linen skirt, red silk blouse, and her usual black high heels. Her blond shoulder-length hair is waved, streaked, and tousled, and she carries a shoulder bag and a stack of papers. No briefcase. "I *never* carry one! I *hate* the way women look lugging them around!"

Entering the Chamber of Commerce building, she gives herself fifteen minutes to greet the men who comprise and dominate the power structure of Colorado. She grabs each one by the arm, draws him close, gives him a hug and a kiss—a real hug, nothing perfunctory. A staff aide of the governor's stops her in the hall. "Don't I get my hug today?"

"Of course you do! Come here, let me get my arms around you! How you doin'?" Barbara Grogan has a soft, cheerful midwestern voice; she grew up in St. Louis, so there's no western twang.

"How are *you*, Barbara?" The governor's man looks

concerned. She had a large tumor removed from her cheekbone the month before, and now she's hiding a vicious scar beneath a pair of big dangling earrings.

"I'm doin' great!" she exults. "Runnin' on twelve cylinders, and I only got ten!"

"You're always great," says another man standing by.

"No, I wasn't *always*. But I'm great now!" You can almost hear the mantra on her dashboard repeating itself in her head: "I am powerful, beautiful, creative, and I can handle it!"

She hurries from the light-filled reception chamber down the stairs to the low-ceilinged basement room, where the Chamber of Commerce's board of directors holds its monthly 7:30 A.M. meeting. Pausing in the anteroom she greets everyone present with gusto, laughing and smiling, moving quickly but not appearing to be in a rush. Above all, she seems to be enjoying herself, with an air of the most popular girl at a dance.

Barbara Grogan introduces a newcomer: "I want you to meet one of my *favorite* people!" When she hears a bit of news she doesn't like, she cries, "Oh, yuck!" With all the smiling and hugging, the words like *yuck* and the hyperbolic adjectives, she's doing everything that women have been told they must never do if they want to be taken seriously as business professionals. But Barbara Grogan has trained herself "not to worry about what people think. The company I've created speaks for itself." She believes that "women have a mission to humanize the workplace by expressing their love, joy, enthusiasm, and caring. And we can't do that unless we are *ourselves*. I made the decision after I started my company that the only way I could succeed and have any fun was by being myself to the *hilt*. I knew I couldn't be one of those women in a dull suit with a little tie, trying to restrain my personality."

The chairman of the Chamber of Commerce board arrives in the basement anteroom. Barbara Grogan hurries to give him the inevitable hug. "I need to talk a bit at the meeting about this," she says. She opens her folder and takes out a clipping from a government magazine about state assistance to small business.

The chairman smiles. "You know I can't refuse you."

She squeezes his arm. "Thanks." Her sharing of "love, joy, enthusiasm, and caring" makes her extremely persuasive.

She takes a doughnut and coffee from the buffet table and moves into the big windowless conference room where the meeting is to take place. Twenty-eight men and five women are seated at four long tables set end-to-end. Barbara Grogan is the last to sit down, but she does not hurry. It is exactly 7:30. Her days are structured down to the minute, but she never gives the impression of being pressured; on the contrary, her disciplined structuring gives her freedom, providing her with the frame in which to "give her moments away."

Because she always knows exactly what she is going to do, and how long she can do whatever she is doing, she feels free to enjoy and really live in the present.

The meeting begins with the chairman's announcement: "Well, we won!" The room breaks into exuberant applause. The previous week, Denver voters passed a referendum authorizing construction of a new $2 billion airport—the first major airport to be built in the United States in twenty years. Members of the chamber campaigned hard for it, convinced that replacing the unreliable Stapleton International Airport was necessary to secure the city's future growth. The people in this room view the referendum as an act of faith in that future, proof that the western spirit is still alive.

The meeting proceeds in a very structured way: opening address, minutes, various reports. A film made to boost the city in its quest to secure the 1992 Olympics is shown. Barbara Grogan makes notes in the pad she has brought along, outlining points to bring up during her next meeting, where she will chair the Governor's Small Business Advisory Council. She explains: "As I've said, I'm careful how I use my minutes. So during a meeting, especially if it's very formal and structured, my attention is 100 percent only if an issue applies to what I'm doing. I'm half listening, and doing something else— writing notes to people, making lists of what I have to do, thinking about a speech I have to give, or even what I'm going to tell my son's teacher in school."

As the film concludes, the chairman calls on Barbara

Grogan for the only bit of business not on the agenda. She remains in her seat and makes her five-minute presentation, speaking indignantly about the article she has clipped on how the various states support small business. "And guess what are the *only* states that don't provide capital to help small business?"

A voice calls out, "Probably Alabama and Colorado."

"That's right! Plus a few other places like Mississippi. And I think it's a disgrace!" She says she plans to photocopy the article, pass it around, make sure the governor sees it, bring it up at the Governor's Advisory Council on Small Business. "In fact, I'm sorry, but I have to leave now to make that meeting."

It is 8:30. She slips out of the room and hurries up the stairs, out into the clear bright day. As she walks the few blocks to the statehouse, she explains that she often leaves such meetings early. "I explain my reasons for leaving, and then get out." It's all part of the discipline she exerts over her schedule. "I prioritize. That means I focus totally on what's most important—what I should be doing to further my most important projects *at this moment*. This often means that I have to leave early or come in at a different time—or make an unscheduled presentation, as I did today." But she points out that prioritizing and structuring need not mean rigidity; the key is to make each decision with full consciousness of big-picture demands. "That way, I can remain spontaneous, respond when something comes up that relates to my larger focus."

115

She reaches the statehouse at 8:50 and passes into the lofty atrium, again stopping to greet everyone she sees. In the conference room where the Governor's Small Business Advisory Council meets, people are gathered around a coffeepot. In all, there are twenty-two people present; half are men, and half are women. The group's job is to advise the governor on policies that relate to small business. There are a variety of committees, and the full group meets once a month.

As small business owners from across the state, the people in this room have a different look than the chamber's executive board members—more western, less button-down. In the earlier meeting, the men wore dark suits, white shirts, and red or yellow ties; here some wear sports shirts and cowboy boots, and the suits are lighter-colored, more shopping mall. The women wear bright suits, white blouses, and white or beige shoes. Their provincial look contrasts with Barbara Grogan's more polished style, which gives her an air of being special.

She lets everyone know that she has just come from the Chamber's monthly board meeting, and that her own newly formed consulting company has just landed a million-dollar contract. She has mastered the ability of informing people of her successes without seeming to brag or appear smug. She manages this by putting a lot of exuberant emotion into her presentation, and proclaiming her own triumphs as victories for everyone. She grabs one man by the arm, tells him about her contract.

"Can you imagine, our little consulting branch is actually *real!* Now we're all on our way!"

Her mention of the Chamber of Commerce draws a few jokes about Denver big shots from those council members who live and do business on Colorado's Western slope, where small towns have been hard hit by the oil bust.

At exactly 9:00 Barbara Grogan raises her voice. "Well, I guess we might as well get this thing started." As chair of the monthly meeting, she takes her place at the head table beside Pat Coyle, the representative from the governor's office. Talking continues as people settle in. There is a kind of constructive disorder, but Barbara Grogan appears in no hurry to exert control.

As voices die down, she calls out, "As difficult as it may be to believe, this group of folks is coming to order!" One man continues talking. "Tom, you come to order too!" Everyone laughs, including Tom. Barbara Grogan's style is that of a friendly teacher, at ease and enjoying herself in the classroom.

"Since our last wonderful day together," she begins, "the executive committee has left a number of things undone." Reading from a sheet of paper, she spells out the agenda for today's meeting. She holds up the article on state aid to small business that she has clipped, summarizes its contents. "I'll make sure everyone gets a copy." She turns to the governor's staffer. "Pat, what's your opinion on this?"

Pat Coyle says that the problem lies with the state

legislature, which restricts funds for capital investment. "I don't see what we can do as long as we've got this bunch in office." His observation leads to a chorus of unhappy complaints about the Republican-controlled state legislature, from Republicans and Democrats alike. Some people gesture and are called on; others just speak out. The meeting begins to meander a bit. Then the mayor of a small mountain town mentions that the Western slope's representative from the state Office of Economic Development has been cut from the budget, and complaints take on a more directed tone. Western slope antagonism, veiled in earlier jokes, surfaces as talk grows more heated. Barbara Grogan sits forward in her chair, her expression intent, fingers running through her hair. She says nothing, occasionally glancing at her watch, but as passions rise, she lets things fly. The small-town mayor sounds angry. "We've got to tell the governor, the state can't *do* this to us! People on the slope feel too cut out of things as it is!"

Others take up the cry. Barbara Grogan continues to listen. She has paper before her, but she doesn't take notes. She waits, then points out that budget cuts have been made across the board. "Any reversal of this policy is highly unlikely. What we're dealing with here is political reality. But I do think these guys"—she nods to the Western slope representatives—"definitely deserve a forum. I'd be glad to draft a letter that says we're very concerned." She makes a note to herself. "I'll do that today. Any last comments? We've got a lot more ground to cover."

Next on the agenda is a discussion of the upcoming visit by the head of the Small Business Administration in Washington. The discussion focuses on details: where should the meeting be held? What committees should make reports? Barbara Grogan takes a few notes, then breaks in. "Wait a minute now, let's really *think* about this one. We should be looking at the big picture. This meeting could be very important! Not just for us, but *nationally.*" She talks about the need to create a model for the whole country—establishing a network for small business, a counseling consortium. "I see this visit as a *giant* opportunity!"

Discussion opens up, moving from petty details to larger ideas. Barbara Grogan breaks in with encouraging comments. *"Now* we're thinking! Let's not waste our big chance." She asks for suggestions, nods excitedly, then suggests a planning committee be formed "to make sure we really use this thing right."

The next topic is the rescheduling of monthly meetings. Barbara Grogan addresses the men and women from the Western slope. "We're sensitive to your travel problems. Help us with the schedule." The talk of timetables that follows again becomes mired in details. "Let's just set a date for the next meeting. Then we can decide on a more permanent schedule. We don't want to get thrown out of this room."

It is now nearly 11:00; the meeting has lasted a full two hours. Barbara Grogan asks for final comments, then declares, "We're out of here!" People stand and stretch. She says her goodbyes with hugs. Then with four other council members, she walks a few blocks to a small natural foods restaurant. "That was *my* kind of meeting!" she exults. *"Flowing!* Not stuffy and by-the-book. The kind of meeting where stuff gets *done."*

Over chicken salad and iced tea, she is full of talk, certainly the dominant figure at the table. She mentions a recent visit to Denver by Mother Teresa and says that, at the same time, a woman who is a Buddhist monk also spoke in the city. "It really excited me to think of *two* women spiritual leaders here in town at the same time. I absolutely believe that the next great spiritual advance in the world is going to come from women." The men at the table, small-town business leaders, nod politely, eyes fixed on their food. They seem unsure what to make of such comments during a business lunch.

Everyone splits the bill, amid jokes about not depleting the Small Business Advisory Council's funds with petty expenses. Barbara Grogan kisses everyone goodbye. She hurries outside to where she has parked her Dodge van. As she wheels out of the parking lot, she presses the digit on the cellular phone that dials her office.

Her secretary answers.

"Hi, Jeanne, I'm in action! Who important called?"

Her secretary lists five names.

120

"Great!" Barbara Grogan says she'll return the call from the governor's chief of staff immediately. "See you soon!"

Heading through downtown, past Civic Center Park with its view of the capitol's gold dome, she makes the call, using the speaker attachment so she doesn't have to pick up the phone. The governor's chief of staff is out. "He and I are playing telephone tag." Leaving a message, she then calls her housekeeper to find out what is happening at home. Her son Ross, aged twelve, seemed a bit unhappy this morning. "Tell him I'll make sure to be home for a bit around four o'clock." She checks about food for the party she is giving at home tonight to celebrate the new contract for terminal design at the airport that her company has won with C.W. Fentriss, a design firm. The housekeeper wants to know how many people will be coming. "I don't know," Barbara Grogan laughs. "Maybe no one will show up! That'd be okay, but we'd better prepare for fifty."

She turns onto the highway, heading west. "I love having this phone," she says. "Last Monday, I had this conference with Ross's teacher at school. I'd hurried away from an important meeting, but the teacher was very late. I had to wait around, and didn't get out until three. I had this big conference call with IBM scheduled—a huge deal, about working with their construction division on a national level. So I just sat there in my van in the schoolyard and dialed the phone. Worked on the deal in the parking lot!"

Ahead, the Rockies are sloped with snow. She identifies the various peaks by name. "Those mountains are my inspiration." Reaching a no-man's-land of industrial parks, a pure Western landscape, she turns onto an access road, crosses a creek, and pulls into a lot. Behind her are prefab houses, a makeshift shack; a few Mexican children and a dog straggle down the road.

It is 12:40 when she reaches the parking lot of her company. These days, it is not unusual for her to arrive this late; she spends about 35 percent of each week on projects outside her company, mostly in meetings or at luncheons. "I don't consider these functions as being extras—they're part of what I do. My job as president is to represent my company in the world and grow it, which means being *out* there, part of what's going on. I meet clients, make connections. The more visible I am, the more visible my company. Also, I'm working to help make this area a better climate for business. I can really see my footprints now, in terms of changing things. The Small Business Profit Center at the chamber services thousands of people a year; that's good for everyone and it's good for me." She believes that joining the Chamber of Commerce is one of the best things she's ever done. "That's what plugged me in to this community."

She walks from the parking lot into the white metal and black glass building to which her company recently moved, stopping to exclaim over the sun on the cottonwoods that grow along the banks of a little creek that flows out back. Western Industrial leases the back half of the long one-story building, and another construction firm leases the front, so the place is filled with men, except for the receptionist and the secretaries.

Jeanne Robinson, Barbara Grogan's secretary, looks concerned when she sees her boss. "Barbara, you really look tired!"

"Do I?" Barbara Grogan runs her fingers through her hair. Her makeup has worn off and the strain of the day is showing. She gets up at 5:30 every morning so that she'll be dressed and ready by the time her children awaken.

She picks up ten pink message slips and carries them into her office, which is in the back corner of the building, separated by head-high partitions. The four men who work directly with her—the controller, the chief estimator, the director of field operations, and the head of her new consulting business—all have their offices "within hollering distance." The ninety or so millwrights, who do the actual moving and installation, work out of field offices that change with every job. The number of these employees also fluctuates according to the amount of business at any given time.

Barbara Grogan takes ten minutes to glance quickly through the mail that Jeanne Robinson has opened and set out on a round table in the center of her office. The walls of the office are covered with awards she has won, both within her industry and for community service, and big blowup photos of outdoor construction sites. A bookcase in the corner holds a few classic business texts and several books by Peter Drucker, and a few paperbacks such as *The Road Less Traveled* by M. Scott Peck. A desk facing the wall is crowded with the framed mottos she uses everyday to keep her spirits high.

> Nothing in the world can take the place of
>   persistence,
> Talent will not; nothing is more common
>   than unsuccessful men with talent.
> Genius will not; unrewarded genius is almost
>   proverbial.
> Education alone will not; the world is full
>   of uneducated derelicts.
> Persistence and determination alone are
>   omnipotent.

And:

> The great pleasure in life is doing
> What people say you cannot do.

These self-help slogans, like the mantra on her dashboard, are important to Barbara Grogan. She started using them at the time of her divorce. "I was a basket case when my husband left me. I had no emotional resources to deal with what had happened. All my values and beliefs were ripped apart. Also, I felt as if I had no *identity:* what was I if I wasn't a wife and mother? For a while, I lived in the Valley of the Damned. I was waiting for something to come along and fix my life. Then it began to sink in: my kids were depending on me—I couldn't sit and wait, I had to fix my life myself."

That realization scared her, but it was also very liberating. "It meant I could stop waiting around." In addition to looking at various ways of earning a living, she knew she had to build self-esteem in order to make it alone in the world. "I was very deliberate about it. I looked on building self-esteem as a task. I had to construct a whole adult personality out of what felt like nothing. So I reached out for anything: I read every self-help book I could get my hands on." Seeing Robert Schuller on television, she sent for his tapes on positive thinking and played them in her car. "Believe me, I wore those suckers out!" She wrote down words and slogans that she felt were helpful and carried them around, developing a habit that has stayed with her. "I'll do anything if it helps keep my confidence and optimism up."

After briefly reading her mail, she sets her message slips by her phone, then sits down for a minute at her desk, thinking silently, blocking out distractions. It is now 1:10, and she wants to be home by 4:00, to talk to her son and prepare for her party tonight. In order to establish priorities, decide what needs to be done in the time remaining, she consults the black Filofax-sized daybook she carries around in her oversized handbag; it contains "everything—from notes about a client I am trying to land to ideas for the grocery list." On each page of the daybook, she has a "things to do" list; as each task is completed, she moves it to the "things done" column on the opposite side of the page.

Based on her list, she decides that her most pressing bit of business is making contact with the new construction head at IBM. The regional IBM manager, whom Barbara Grogan met through the Chamber of Commerce, has informed her that IBM will be entering a new business—the full-service development of office space. IBM will buy land for a client, build the plant, and buy and install the equipment, subcontracting the specialized work. If she moves fast, Barbara Grogan sees a chance to get in on the ground floor of a potentially enormous venture.

She pulls a gray spiral notebook from the bookcase beside her desk, opens it, and dials the phone. Using the regional manager's name, she gets the head of the new venture on the phone. "Don's been telling me about what you're doing, and I'm very excited!" she says. "And I want to tell you why I think your venture and my company might be a great fit." She asks for more information. "Could you please tell me about your rules and goals? Exactly the kind of project you're going to be encompassing?"

She listens intently to the response, making fast notes in her gray spiral notebook. She uses these notebooks to keep a record of the substance of every business phone call she either makes or receives. She dates each entry, and keeps them organized according to date.

"That way, I can check, see when I made a given call, then refresh myself on exactly what was said." She likes to check the notebook file before making a call to someone with whom she talks irregularly, so she can refer to the specifics of "our last call."

Now, as the IBM construction head finishes talking, she says, "Let me tell you something about us." She describes the precision work her company does, names a few clients, mentions the airport contract her consulting branch just landed. "We do lots of things I'd love to tell you about. We work all over the country, and our reputation is *impeccable*. People will tell you two things about us: that we get the job done, and that we have the highest level of integrity." She says she'll send some material over. "And then may I call you back in ten days? Great! It's been wonderful talking to you!"

The phone call has lasted a full half hour.

Hanging up, she springs from her desk and hurries to the table; her eyes roll heavenward, and she cries out, "Thank you!" The conversation with the IBM engineer has activated her optimism, and the exhaustion her secretary noted on her face vanishes. "This business is poised on the edge of extraordinary things. I can just *feel* it!" She calls out to her secretary over the low partition. "Jeanne! Could you pop in here for a sec?"

The secretary steps into the office. Barbara Grogan jots down the name and address of the man from IBM. "Send this guy over a packet *immediately*. No, hold on a minute—I'm going to write him a personal note as well.

And please buzz Kent to see if he can come into my office."

Kent Stutsman is the head of the consulting division that Barbara Grogan started to market estimating and scheduling services on large construction jobs that might encompass more than Western Industrial's specialty of millwrighting. She decided to offer the service because she wanted to expand her business, but didn't want to dilute the company's image or reputation by moving into other kinds of construction.

As she waits, Barbara Grogan returns to the round table where her mail has been laid out, picks up three letters and moves them onto her desk. Then Kent Stutsman steps into her office. "Hi, Kent! You got a minute?"

He sits down beside her at the round center table. "Sure."

Barbara Grogan tells him about her phone call with the IBM engineer. "I'm going to write the guy as *soon* as you leave my office. This thing could be really big. When IBM does something, they really *do* it!" She summarizes the Chamber board meeting she attended this morning. "The whole business community is so excited about this airport. And we're part of it!"

Kent Stutsman is with Barbara Grogan for fifteen minutes. No particular business is discussed. The meeting is just about keeping in touch, keeping enthusiasm high. She explains, "I rarely have formal meetings in my company, and my people have a lot of freedom and autonomy. Since they don't report in any formal sense, keeping in touch is very important. So I use a lot of very short—often just ten-minute—informal get-togethers. Sometimes it's just a way of saying, 'You're important to me,' reaffirming our connection. It makes my people feel good, and it makes me feel good too."

It is 2:10 when Kent Stutsman leaves the office. Barbara Grogan takes out a yellow legal pad and begins drafting a letter to the construction head at IBM. She writes all correspondence in longhand, then has her secretary type up the letters. "My mail is very important to me. I'm careful to answer it promptly. And I believe in *personal*, not form, letters. Plus, I never dictate. I've tried, but it just doesn't work. I have to see my words, correct as I go." She does keep a dictating machine in her car, but she uses it only for thinking aloud and recording ideas. "I'll remind myself of things I have to do, then play the tape back and schedule those things in my daybook."

The letter takes fifteen minutes. At 2:25 she calls her secretary in again. "Take this and include it in the packet you're sending to the IBM guy. Plus, let him have an updated client list." She rummages in a desk drawer until she finds one.

The secretary returns to her own desk, after handing Barbara Grogan three more message slips—calls that came in while she was on the phone or with Kent Stutsman. She has now spent just over an hour on the item of business she decided was a priority: initiating ties with a new client, following up on the initial contact, and disseminating the news to the relevant person in her company. She has taken it as far as she can. Now she turns to the three pieces of mail she moved onto her desk.

The first is a request from a small business group inviting her to speak next month at its forum. "I'll answer this one right away," she says to herself. She sits down, scratches out another letter on the legal pad. Writing it takes her fifteen minutes. She spends substantial time in her office broadening the ties that bind her to many segments of the world. "I see it as a strong part of what I do—keeping my name and my company's name out there."

As she is finishing the letter, the head of field operations, Mike Barnes, appears in the doorway. "Hi, Mike!" He comes in, sprawls in a chair. He is wearing scuffed boots and jeans, and speaks with a western twang.

As with Kent Stutsman, there doesn't seem to be a particular purpose to this meeting—it is more a way of keeping in touch. Barbara Grogan asks how the company is doing on the Denver Rapid Transit Development, a huge bus maintenance plant where it is installing equipment.

"Well, I'm still lookin' for a crane and a forklift," says Mike Barnes. "Plus those trenches are still in place." He is referring to trenches dug by the contractor on a previous job that are now preventing Western Industrial from moving equipment onto the construction site.

130

"Just tell me," says Barbara Grogan. "Is this something you're worried about?"

"Not really."

"Okay, then. I know you can handle it."

Barbara Grogan gives her employees great autonomy. "I don't know how to do their jobs, and I don't pretend I do. I'm the chief executive of this company, I drum up business, and I set the vision, but I don't supervise operations. If I hire someone, why would I think I could do a better job than he could? My guiding principle is to pick the right people, and then trust 'em. I do think you learn a lot about trusting people from being a mother. You have to let kids make their own mistakes if you want them to develop. And doing that is a lot harder than giving adults who work with you autonomy!"

Barbara Grogan continues her chat with Mike Barnes. "By the way, I had this dream last night. The foreman on that job out there told me he was going to retire. I woke up and realized—I think he'd better start training a second-in-command."

"Good idea," says Mike Barnes. "You're probably right." He does not seem surprised that this decision should have come to Barbara Grogan in a dream. Later, she explains, "I've worked with my guys long enough; they've learned to ride with my instincts. They know I rely on my gut, and they've seen that I'm right a lot. Even when it sounds nutty, like with a dream."

Mike Barnes leaves her office at 3:00. She has been with him for twenty minutes. She decides that the two letters she had put aside will have to wait; if she writes replies, she won't have time to return her phone calls. Her talks with her employees, both spontaneous, assumed priority. "All that means is that I cycle these letters back to being less important." She notes their revised status by putting them in the to-do column of her daybook.

But one letter must be done today: a recounting to the governor's chief of staff of the high points of this morning's meeting. She opens the folder she had with her this morning, and turns to the sketchy notes she made during that meeting; working from them, she composes her letter in fifteen minutes. She includes a warning in the letter that "The people on the Western slope feel abandoned." It is a stronger statement of concern than she had promised to make during the meeting. "The frustration those people expressed had a chance to sink in on me," she explains. "I speak for them to the governor. I have to make their feelings heard."

Randy Baker, her controller, appears in the doorway, and she gestures for him to come in. Holding out a stack of checks, he asks, "Should we hold on to these for a bit, or send them out?"

Barbara Grogan shuffles through the pile. "Send 'em. We got the money, send 'em out." She begins to sign the checks quickly, by hand. "Also, send out those bills you got. One of them is to IBM, and they pay quickly!" She talks to Randy Baker about what a great company IBM is to work for. "They pay their bills on time, no questions, no messing around. So contractors love to work for them, and do their best. They fit in with my belief about what goes around comes around."

Randy Baker slips out of the office. Barbara Grogan spends fifteen minutes returning "the really *key* calls" that came in that morning. She greets each person with great enthusiasm, encouragement, and compliments: "Hi! I got tons of comments on that great speech of yours last night!" Or, "Thanks for being so prompt about returning my phone call. How *are* you? Oh, that makes me happy to hear!"

By 3:40 she has made five calls; though each had a casual conversational feel, none lasted more than three or four minutes. After glancing one last time through her messages, she consults her daybook and concludes, "Nothing else really has to be done today. This is what I mean by pacing myself. I do what I can and don't try to cram things in. If something doesn't get done, I leave it alone. My housekeeper said my son had something worrying him, so going home early became my priority, and whatever I felt could wait had to wait."

She calls Jeanne Robinson in again, and gives her the letters she has just written, to the small business group asking her to speak and to the governor's chief of staff. She asks her to type and send them out. "One more thing." She gives her the article on state assistance to small business that she's been carrying around all day. "I need a bunch of photocopies. Now, I'm out of here!"

In her Dodge van, Barbara Grogan phones her housekeeper, tells her she's on the way home. She just has to stop and pick up the champagne she's ordered for tonight's party. A call comes in from her sixteen-year-old daughter Holly, who seems excited to be talking to her mother on the car phone. Holly says she's on her way to her after-school waitressing job. "Oh, too bad!" says Barbara Grogan. "You'll miss the party."

After buying the champagne, Barbara Grogan spends forty-five minutes at home, giving attention to her twelve-year-old son. Building personal or family breaks into her work routine is not unusual. "I try to be home every night by six. If there's a cocktail party, I always leave early. My evenings belong to my kids. But on those nights when I can't be home at six, I usually stop home during the day, so I can be there when they get home from school." In addition, Barbara Grogan almost never goes into the office on weekends; nor does she encourage employees to work nights or weekends. "I don't reward workaholism. My employees have families too, and those families are important."

By 5:00 she is headed back downtown. Her makeup is fresh, and she is wearing an elegant navy knit dress with gold jewelry. Her plan is to make a quick run-through of the Chamber of Commerce's annual year-end cocktail party before returning home to host her own celebration.

Parking her van in front of the Denver Marriott, she slips her handbag beneath the front seat. She makes a point of never carrying a purse to social functions. "It seems nerdy to arrive at these things with a purse. You're always clutching it, or worrying where to put it. You don't see men encumbered by big heavy pouches!"

At the entrance to the huge downstairs room where the party is being held, Barbara Grogan pauses to survey the scene. She knows she has only a half hour, but she is going to enjoy it. She sees the former chairman of the chamber's executive board, a white-haired man with a Texas accent. She hugs him in delight. "Rex!"

Other men join them. Everywhere, there are groups of men. The few other women are dressed in bright or pastel suits and white shoes; their clothes are wrinkled from the day. In her fresh dark dinner dress, Barbara Grogan looks polished. Not carrying a purse works for her too—the other women *do* look hampered, anxious. Unencumbered, she is like the CEO who arrived at a function by limousine, and so is the only person in the room not clutching a raincoat.

As she moves eagerly through the crowd to greet people, she has the air of someone at ease with her own power. Though not beautiful, she has the magnetism of a woman in her prime—aware, confident, assertive, clearly enjoying herself, bold enough to break the rules when she wants to. She knows how to be affectionate to the men around her without diminishing her own dignity, without even suggesting any kind of come-on. Her radiant sexuality is maternal. She stops as she moves through the room to straighten an occasional tie.

Barbara Grogan's essential style—at this cocktail party, as at the governor's meeting she chaired this morning—is that of a warm and popular teacher.

It is this attitude that enables her to get away with all her hugging. "I greet everyone with hugs," she explains. "That's part of what I mean about being myself. It took people a while to accept it. When I first joined the chamber in 1984, the guys didn't know what to make of me. Who was this weird woman, always hugging everyone? Didn't she know enough to act professional? But I told myself not to care, they'd get used to it. I wasn't going to let men determine all the rules! Now, they not only like it, they expect it. Did you see that guy this morning who came up to me, 'Where's my hug?' I love that. *I love it!* It shows I'm making a change in the way these men respond. They're opening up, seeing that things can be done in different ways. It makes them feel good. It makes me feel good too. It makes the feminine presence here more pronounced."

This is Barbara Grogan's last day as the Chamber board member in charge of the Small Business Project. Next year, she will direct the membership committee. Now, as a man in a bow tie passes, she reaches out and grabs him. "Charlie! I've *got* to talk to you!" She takes him by the arm, steers him aside. "I told everyone, I won't even *think* about chairing membership unless you agree to be on my committee."

Charlie in the bow tie smiles. "Well, as a start, how about we make a commitment to double membership within a year?"

"I knew it! That's why I need you on the committee. You think *big*, just like me!"

Although the membership committee won't begin formal meetings until fall, Barbara Grogan suggests she and Charlie meet for lunch the following week so they can get a start on hatching their plans.

She moves away, helps herself to a club soda, then spends ten more minutes circulating, greeting everyone with hugs and repeating her conversation with Charlie. She checks her watch. It is almost 6:00; she has been here nearly an hour. She begins saying quick goodbyes. "I never spend more than an hour at these things," she declares as she threads through the mazelike parking garage to her van. "Sometimes I go to four a week, but I never stay very long."

As she drives home, she reiterates; "My evenings belong to my kids. We eat dinner together, then maybe go for a bike ride—there are these wonderful bicycle paths near my house." Barbara Grogan finishes her evenings with reading. "I watch *no* TV, so I read every night." She likes mysteries and thrillers, psychological self-help and especially "spiritual books—food for my mind and my soul."

Her thoughts turn to the party she has just attended, and to the one she is giving tonight. "The people we just saw were the movers and shakers in this town. The people at my party will be the worker bees, the ones who get things *done*. And the thing is, I love talking to them all. I guess I just love talking to people—that's what keeps me going."

She parks in front of the large, comfortable brick house where she moved when she was still married, on a shady street in a well-kept older part of town. It's 6:10 and she wonders aloud if any of her guests will be there. "I can't remember if I told people six or seven."

She hurries inside, but no one has arrived yet. The housekeeper has set up the dining table—platters full of fruit, shrimp, and cold cuts. Barbara Grogan surveys it, nibbles a bit, then sits down in the living room to talk with her son. "Maybe we'll be lucky," she tells him. "maybe nobody will come."

But at 7:00 the bell begins to ring and she's at the door, greeting guests. Without being told, her son asks people if he can get them champagne. By 8:00 the house is filled with people toasting the new consulting company's contract at the airport. This being the construction business, the crowd is mostly men—architects, engineers, designers, lawyers. About half have brought their wives. Most of the wives work; everyone knows one another. It's a lively crowd, and people are slow to leave.

But by 10:30 Barbara Grogan is tired. She has been up since 5:30 and will be up at that time tomorrow, spending time with her kids before starting her workday. Although a core of guests is still talking in her kitchen, she starts putting the champagne back in the refrigerator, asking two men to help her clear what is left of the food. A wife whispers to her husband, "She's putting stuff away! She wants us *out* of here." Barbara Grogan, overhearing, smiles and nods sleepily. With her shoes off, wrapping ham and cheese at the kitchen counter, she could be any weary hostess who has the confidence to assert her need to go to bed. But as her hands move, she is still telling people about her plans to double membership in the Chamber of Commerce. "I told Charlie, he thinks like me. *Big!*"

CHAPTER SIX

Breaking Down Boundaries:

Nancy Badore,
Ford Motor Company

Nancy Badore is constantly modeling behavior that breaks down status distinctions and confounds expectations of executive attitudes and comportment. She seeks to empower those around her by being direct and natural in a way that minimizes her own ego and strips herself of the trappings of power that emphasize boundaries and hierarchical divisions. She is willing to court a certain amount of criticism or condescension in order to achieve this almost sacrificial purpose. It is a consequence of her unceasing search for ways to coax forth information and forge new alliances by "not letting my role get in my way."

Nancy Badore is the executive director of the Ford Motor Company's Executive Development Center, which is responsible for training the company's top two thousand managers worldwide in the "new culture" values based on quality and customer orientation. It is this new culture that is credited with enabling Ford to emerge from its near collapse in the early eighties and stage a spectacular comeback, earning all-time record profits by

1987. In the process of resurrecting itself, Ford has become almost a paradigm of the reinvented corporation, although on an unusually massive scale. The company has begun dismantling by increments its rigid hierarchical structure organized around competing and isolated fiefdoms, and has instituted a participative team approach that focuses total attention on the final product. The change has presented a challenge to psyches as well as systems, and in this Nancy Badore has played an instrumental role.

Now forty-three years old, she joined the company in 1979, a watershed year in Detroit's history. Declining sales, customer discontent, defective products, and angry workers were finally forcing American automakers to confront the need for change. Nancy Badore, with a Ph.D. in psychology, took a position on the corporate employee relations staff, where she worked on establishing Ford's Employee Involvement program, the first step in the company's effort at self-transformation.

The original idea behind Employee Involvement was to get union stewards and plant managers past their antagonistic, us-versus-them presumptions so they could start talking to one another. One of Ford's biggest problems at that time was that managers rarely talked to subordinates, much less to superiors or colleagues in other divisions. Information flowed *up*, beginning on the plant floor and extending throughout the company. Each aspect of car making—design, product planning, engineering, manufacturing, sales—was run as an entity unto itself by people insulated from one another in their own narrowly defined areas of specialization. This vertically coordinated "chimney system," as it was called, with its emphasis on rigid boundaries, prevailed throughout the auto business in Detroit.[1]

Nancy Badore says, "I came into Employee Involvement as a junior member, one of those bright-eyed people who come into the plant and say, 'Hi, I'm from staff and I'm here to help you.' We really didn't know *what* we were doing, the whole field was new—there was little literature on the organizational change on this scale, so we had to feel our way. The plants became laboratories in which we tried different techniques to break down boundaries, get people contributing—to see what motivated them to work with zest and spirit. I was on that team that went from plant to plant, and I became fascinated with what we were learning; pretty soon I became sort of a Dear Abby on practical hints about implementing culture change."

As Employee Involvement succeeded in opening up communications on the plant floor and getting people focused on product quality, a new problem began to arise. Plant management teams were becoming more progressive than their respective division heads who were still steeped in the old hierarchical culture. In the mid-eighties, Nancy Badore took charge of a project to bring division heads together with plant managers, so that division managers could listen to and learn from them. "It was unpopular—the idea of executives learning from programs developed in the plant. The whole notion was considered inappropriate, and I came in for my share of hostility," Nancy Badore recalls. But the program worked so well that her next assignment was to develop a model for a permanent structure within Ford that would train the company's "generals and colonels" in the new culture, and keep training them on a continuing basis.

The model Nancy Badore crafted became the Executive Development Center (EDC), a semiautonomous, fully funded entity with an anomalous position within Ford's structure. As executive director, Nancy Badore reports to an executive vice president just below the chairman; this, and the fact that the EDC educates the very top layer of managers and plays a pivotal role in defining the direction of change, give it an importance and influence far out of proportion to its nineteen-person staff and operating budget in the $5 million range.

The EDC's mandate is to keep executives "talking up the ladder"—questioning both business specialists and company officers who teach various courses, so that this assertive behavior will carry over after an executive has completed the training. The entire program is focused on the need to break down the boundaries that divide and segment management, and lessen the hushed aura of respect that insulates top management at a huge corporation like Ford.

146

Nancy Badore strides onto the thirty-eighth floor of Detroit's downtown Renaissance tower where the EDC has two floors. She moves quickly, greeting people in her strong voice, carrying a large envelope but still managing to gesture with her hands. "Good morning, madam!" she calls to a receptionist, then leans into the offices of the program directors, all male, who form her team: "Good morning! Hello!" She is a tall, thin woman with an arresting air of confidence and brisk, athletic movements. Her graying blond hair is pulled back into a ponytail, and she wears black pants and low black shoes, a black-and-white silk blouse, red woven jacket, and a red-and-yellow silk scarf. Her nails are unmanicured and her gold jewelry low key, except for a huge Japanese fan pin. The effect is tasteful, but strongly individual and even flamboyant.

She moves into her own office, a huge sweeping room with a wide desk, curved corner sofa, round meeting table, and a wall of windows showing the Detroit River and Canada beyond. Her secretary, Dee Durocher, comes in and hands her the day's agenda, a computer printout, and a $5'' \times 3''$ pink file card with several more meetings typed in.

Nancy Badore scans the agenda, nods, and slips it into a black Filofax-sized daybook. Each morning, Dee Durocher presents her with an agenda; the printout shows not only the current day's schedule, but the schedule for the preceding and following days as well. Nancy Badore's calendar is in her secretary's charge.

"I'm not that good with sticking to schedules," she explains. "Dee keeps me organized."

Nancy Badore asks Dee to sit down with her at the big round worktable. She sets down the envelope she has been carrying and pulls out a manuscript, the work of an author who is doing a book on changing management styles. Two of the chapters are on Ford, and Nancy Badore has been prominently featured; the author sent the chapters to her and she read them over last night. "There are a lot of inaccuracies. I need to write the author a letter."

It is now 8:40. Dee Durocher opens her notebook. Nancy Badore glances at the notes she made last night on lined graph paper. She pauses, gathering her thoughts, then begins offering suggestions to the author, telling him the various people he should talk to while doing revisions. She makes her points in full sentences, including the commas and the stops, as her secretary takes it all down in shorthand.

"I never used dictation until Dee and I crossed paths," Nancy Badore explains. "I got to be a manager without ever learning how to do it. I used to draft my own letters, really work over them. Then I hooked up with Dee, and she likes doing it this way, and I discovered that I prefer it too. I think about the letter, compose it in my mind, take a few notes, and then talk it out. I'm oriented to be very verbal, so this is a more natural channel for me than writing."

The dictation lasts ten minutes. At 8:50, a call comes in. Dee Durocher takes it in her office. "It's John Tavalyn, calling from Brazil."

"Tavalyn, Tavalyn—I'm blanking on the name," says Nancy Badore. But she moves to her big desk and takes the phone. She listens, then begins to nod. John Tavalyn is a Ford executive in Brazil; he is wondering if the EDC would be interested in sponsoring a session in São Paulo. "That sounds exciting, John! Yes, we've taken courses on the road. They're cost-effective and can be given to whole teams—sometimes the enthusiasm that that generates works wonders." She listens. "What's *your* feeling?" She glances at her watch. "I'd love to keep talking about this, but I'm late for a nine o'clock meeting." She continues to listen, however, then finally cuts it short. Scribbling a note to herself, she hurries from the office.

In the outer room, she glances at some empty plates set out on a table. "Great! I see all the strawberries are gone." She has begun a policy of keeping fresh fruit in various spots around the EDC offices. "Without getting too big brotherish about it, we're trying to encourage the health thing."

She steps into the large circular lobby around which the offices are grouped; here the executives who are taking the various EDC training programs gather between sessions. A large table is set up with fruit, coffee, cereals, oat bran muffins, and boiled eggs. Nancy Badore nods approvingly—more evidence of the "health thing"—but grabs two diet Cokes to get her through the meeting.

She hurries upstairs to the Ford Room, a huge corporate conference room with an enormous center table, a marble fireplace, and floor-to-ceiling windows that give a view north to Lake St. Clair. She is ten minutes late for the monthly meeting of her management team of program managers. Six of the seven are waiting; the seventh is "deaning" this week, leading the executive training session taking place. All the program managers are men; they are dressed conventionally in solid-color shirts and ties, except for a single case of subdued plaid. In her red jacket, Nancy Badore is the only spot of color.

She has explained on the way up. "This meeting has two purposes. The first is to give the program managers exposure to one another's projects and ideas. They're not briefing me, that's not what this is about. The second purpose is to bring John Walker up-to-date." She explains that he is the new member of the team, and will be working directly with her, in charge of operations and planning. The idea is to free her from the day-to-day administrative work that comes with running her division. "It's a balancing act. I brought him in to be the sane one, so I can be the crazy one in this organization."

It is not unusual for Nancy Badore to describe herself as "crazy." What exactly does she mean? "It has to do with giving myself permission to be fully me, which is the only way I can be creative and spark creativity in others. Being crazy is also not letting my role here get in the way of being able to learn what I need to know. Not becoming so conscious of having an executive image in the company that I start pretending I know what I don't. Being crazy means I let myself ask even really stupid questions. And I *have* to do that, because it's something I try to encourage around this place. When executives come in for the training programs, they're often reluctant to ask questions or challenge speakers, because they don't want to look like idiots. If we want to get them talking *up* the ladder—sharing their ideas, not being afraid—we've got to get them past all that. One thing *I* can do is use myself as an example. They see I'm not afraid to look ridiculous, and that helps to set the tone. I'm very conscious of using myself as a model in this way, knowing full well that these guys might attribute the way I act to my being a female."

Now she takes her place at the head of the conference table and snaps open a diet Coke. "Sorry I'm late. I have a copy of the agenda somewhere." She rummages in her notebook. "Here! Okay, David, I think you're the one to start."

David Murphy, a young but gray-haired Irishman, is one of two people in charge of the Senior Executive Program, or SEP, a five-and-a-half-day course for fifty executives that every one of Ford's top two thousand must go through every two years. It is the core program around which the EDC revolves. He hands around a thick agenda for his presentation, with major points printed in huge type.

As he leafs through it, elaborating the points, he addresses himself to Nancy Badore and to John Walker, the new head of operations and planning. Several times, Nancy Badore breaks in; always, she seems to be broadening the discussion. As she listens, she leans back in her chair, almost sprawling, gesturing with her hands. When David Murphy speaks of "BIC" and "P&SC," she turns to John Walker, who is newly arrived from England. "Please tell us when we're using U.S. acronyms! The important thing at this meeting is for *you* to understand." When David Murphy gives his report on "customer care"—how well the groups of executives are cared for during their stay in Detroit—she asks pointed questions: "How about the hotel? Any complaints? What more can we do? Suggestions from anyone on how we can make this better?" With her probing, she is "modeling" the process of talking up the ladder—encouraging those present to offer suggestions although the points addressed are beyond their area of specialization.

John Wood, David Murphy's co-chair on SEP, now takes over, and the discussion turns to the speakers who teach the various courses. Some of them are not satisfactory. Nancy Badore asks, "Are some of these guys coachable?"

There is general agreement that one in particular is difficult. John Wood says to Nancy Badore, "I think you recognized there might be problems with him at the start."

"I did. And you know, I usually rely a lot on my

intuition, but in this case we all ignored our feelings. There's a lesson in there. I think the key is, when we audition these guys we shouldn't focus on how much they know. We've got to ask ourselves, what would it be like to *learn* from this person? When we think like that, we'll be more apt to anticipate participants' reactions. Instead of thinking he *must* be good because he's so brilliant, and hoping that he'll be more effective than he comes across to us."

She talks of the need to structure more lulls into the SEP training program. "It's during breakouts that things really get done." Nancy Badore is a great believer in "breakouts" during training sessions, relatively unstructured times when those in training can relax and share ideas. "You can't keep people occupied all the time. You've got to trust them to be on their own, treat them like they've got brains. A lot of the most valuable stuff comes from interplay among colleagues. They find someone else agrees with their ideas, and that strengthens them. They feel better about challenging the speaker when they get into the next instruction session, and *that's* what talking up the ladder is all about."

It is 9:50. A secretary knocks on the door to say that Allan Gilmour has called; he's the executive Vice President for Corporate Staffs. Nancy Badore excuses herself and hurries to return the call. "We now report through Allan," she explains, "and he's taken a close interest in what we're doing here."

She finds an empty office nearby and dials, but Allan

Gilmour is out. She leaves a message, then calls Dee Durocher to ask her to put the call through to the conference room. "I want to take only the most important calls during a meeting."

She returns as the SEP review is finishing up. When John Wood finishes speaking, she turns to John Walker and summarizes briefly for him what she considers critical in the discussion so far. "The most important criterion here, as with all the programs, is *does it make a difference* to the corporation? Not just *does it make a good class?*" She keeps reiterating, "We've got to keep the big picture in mind. Of course the details matter, but we can't get lost in the details."

She says it is time to move on to the next item on the agenda, "but since it's already ten, let's take a short break."

She hurries downstairs to her office and immediately telephones her father-in-law, who is at her home caring for her twenty-two-month-old baby. "We're really lucky—when my husband's father, Bernie, retired, he moved out here from California to help take care of Maggie."

There is no answer on the phone. "He's probably at the doctor's or the drugstore." She explains that the baby has the flu. She leaves a message on the answering machine. "Did Maggie's apple juice go down okay? What's her temperature? Please call me as soon as you get back to the house!"

She goes out to check her messages with Dee Durocher. Four calls have come in. "These can wait. Just two calls I want put through—Allan Gilmour and Bernie!"

Dee Durocher hands her copy of the letter to the author that she had dictated earlier. Nancy Badore pens a few corrections: "Okay, print it." She hurries from the office. Passing the food table, she expresses disappointment that the fruit remains untouched while the chocolate chip cookies have been "zeroed in on." She takes her third diet Coke of the morning, then grabs an oat bran muffin. "This thing is so awful, it's got to be healthy."

The men are waiting when she enters the room, munching on her muffin. "Okay, smarties, what's next? The Associations Program?" She sits down and looks at Dick Hartshorn, the man in the plaid shirt, who is passing around his agenda. "All right, Mr. Guru, tell us what's going on."

The Associations Program is a series of seminars for Ford executives doing business with Japan and Korea; it will be broadened to include other countries as well. As Dick Hartshorn makes his presentation, Nancy Badore listens intently, making an occasional note, reminding him when he uses jargon to "watch those acronyms!"

At one point, when Dick Hartshorn is talking about input the Association programs have been receiving from Ford executives who have done business in Seoul, Nancy Badore breaks in. "I think we've really got to look at this. We've got excellent teachers, but we've got to find better ways to structure in what the guys in the training sessions have to say." She turns to John Walker: *"They're* the ones who are out there in the field. I see a Marco Polo analogy here. It's as if the company has given these guys a charter. They're going on the expeditions, picking up new data about what the world is like. Since they're out there, we need to be listening to them! We don't want to be talking *at* them, we want to be learning *from* them. What's it like to do business in a newly industrialized country? What sorts of things earn a Korean's trust? We've got to structure these programs to be a two-way learning process."

This is one of Nancy Badore's favorite themes. Later, she explains, "When you have a program like the EDC, it doesn't work if you only teach. You also have to gather information from the executives being taught." She observes that the whole notion behind Employee Involvement was to promote a *diversity* of means of exchange, rather than limiting information to something that flowed up and down prescribed channels. It involved opening many links, eliminating boundaries. "So now, if we only have information going from teachers to students, we'll just be replicating the old top-down process."

The presentation ends at 10:50. Nancy Badore points out that they are supposed to have reached this point on the agenda at 10:00. Still, she doesn't cut the discussion short. People have taken up her Marco Polo analogy, and are volunteering bits of information about what Ford may face doing business in Communist countries. There is excitement at the prospect of a whole new world of markets. Nancy Badore interjects, "Just so we remember you can't predict these things. A few months ago, everything looked like a go-ahead for U.S. business in China."

She thanks Dick Hartshorn. "On to you, Vic!" she says, turning to Victor Leo, who heads Strategic Decision Making, a three-day program offered to small groups of executives. As he hands his agenda to John Walker, Nancy Badore gets up to throw away her three Coke cans; a few minutes later, she turns down the air conditioner. She moves around more than any of the men; she also laughs more, and her gestures are larger. They sit for the most part with their hands in their pockets, while she fools with the bow holding her ponytail. With her red jacket, big pin, and colorful scarf, she seems to relish her visibility, to glory in her unself-consciousness, her inability and refusal to blend in, her deliberate rejection of status behavior and symbols.

Again, she periodically cuts into the discussion, always widening it, putting the big picture in focus. "We have to keep in mind," she says, "what this strategic thinking course is really about. The integration of all the *parts* of the company. Not the maximum functioning of the individual parts!" And later: "One of the things we need to be thinking about is marketing these courses better, ensuring that people who can benefit from them are aware they are available. I heard one of these guys

157

(the course teachers) saying he didn't want to be in the position of 'peddling a course.' That's wrong thinking—as wrong as you can get! These programs are our product!"

At 10:30 the phone in the conference room rings, and Nancy Badore hurries to answer it. While the men at the table continue to discuss strategic thinking, she leans against the wall and talks. "Is it aspirin-based? She kept it down? Oh, wonderful! Yes, that's what I'd do. Maggie doesn't *like* raspberry flavor. Thanks so much for calling, I needed to know."

She comes back in on the meeting as Vic Leo is talking about the need for more specific feedback from the courses. "We need to get beyond the 'hey, I was blown away' rhetoric." She laughs appreciatively, then, noting it is 11:00, suggests another ten-minute break.

While the men file out for coffee, she telephones Dee Durocher from the conference room and asks her to reschedule her 11 A.M. meeting to 11:30. Then she talks to me about how delightful it is, learning about parenting at the age of forty-two. She mentions her other daughter, her first, now in her early twenties, whom she and her husband gave up for adoption when they were both seventeen. "We'd both just started college and we didn't know what else to do. Back in those days, adoption was presented as the only choice. All the counselors gave you the Cinderella answers—you were doing the best thing for your child, she would have a wonderful home with wonderful loving parents. Unspoken, of course, was the idea that you'd been a little tramp, and had to pay for your sins by giving up your baby."

So Nancy Badore and her husband (then her boyfriend) gave up their little girl, and after college they got married. Her career progressed, but in her thirties, when she began wanting a child, she found herself unable to become pregnant. Thinking of the child she had given up, she got in touch with a birth parents' advocacy group, and she and her husband undertook a search for their daughter. Four years ago, they found her, attending college in Florida; they flew down and were reunited. "It was so unbelievable, so wonderful! And that week, *the week we found her*—that was the week I conceived Maggie." It was as if a dam had burst—a dam of longing for her lost child, and she was finally able to be a mother again.

Nancy Badore talks freely about this extraordinary experience as the men return to the meeting. It is difficult to tell if they are embarrassed by her openness, her breaking of boundaries between the public and private realms. She says she has been criticized for bringing her baby to the office when she works on Sundays. "Some of the men think it's not professional, not the right image for an executive, but I'm trying to get people past that kind of thinking. Having a baby around—besides being important for *me*—helps loosen these guys up, makes them more responsive. And it sends a message that we think the *whole* person is valuable around here. That means the person as he relates to his family, not just his work. Work and family are part of who you *are!"*

When everyone is seated, David Murphy hands around the agenda for the Corporate Executive Program, a series of courses for executives who have recently been promoted. "We've only got half an hour, and you get half of that," says Nancy Badore. Once, when she tries to cut in with a remark, David Murphy laughingly objects. "Boss, you're stealing my time!" He shares a story that a senior executive told during one of the sessions about coming near to an emotional collapse early in his career as a result of pushing himself too hard. The tale ends with a moral about the need to achieve balance between work and family. "I don't think I've heard real stories related so meaningfully before," says Nancy Badore. *"That's* what we're looking for." She agrees with David Murphy that the interview session from which the story emerged should be continued as part of the EDC's seminar material.

At 11:45 David Murphy finishes his report. Nancy Badore gets up and excuses herself, saying she must find the women on her staff with whom she has already rescheduled an 11:00 meeting, and try to reschedule it again. As she hurries downstairs, she explains that she is letting the present meeting go yet another half hour because the next report due is from the newest member of the program management team: "I don't want him to feel slighted by my saying we're out of time."

160

She finds the two staffers, Mary Aughton and Janice Turowski, with whom she was supposed to meet. "I came down here to offer my personal apologies," she says. "Should we try to find a different day, or do you mind changing your luncheon?" The women agree that changing lunch presents no problem, and say they'll be in Nancy Badore's office by 12:15. "Thanks so much for your understanding," she says, and hurries off. She is their boss but, as she points out, "I wouldn't feel right to keep sending messages like that through my secretary. I need to be considerate of their time."

Back in the meeting, Al Solvay, the new manager on the team, is discussing the leadership seminars, telling John Walker how he came to be in charge. He explains that when he first met the teacher of the seminars, he found him difficult, too focused on money. "I told Nancy, and she said, 'Go ahead and share that feeling with him.' She pointed out that the guy put great stock in honesty, and would want to know what I had to say even though it was critical. So I went back and told him what was bothering me, and we decided to work on it together. And when I told Nancy, she said, 'Great, I'm putting you in charge of the program!' "

"See, there's a case where I went with my instinct," she says. "And my instinct turned out to be right. Al has the ability to be utterly candid without making people defensive. He saved the course."

A discussion follows on the material taught in the seminars. Then at 12:10 Nancy Badore cuts it off.

"We *must* spend five minutes on something very important—that is, this question of marketing ourselves." She is referring to the EDC brochure, now in the planning stages. Al Solvay passes a prototype around. There is a brief weighing of its merits. Nancy Badore warns, "We've learned from Al's research that we've got to be careful about not designing for obsolescence. We need a brochure that can accommodate us in *change.*"

It is nearly 12:25. Nancy Badore stands up. "I have *got* to go to my next meeting!" She turns to John Wood, the other member of the team who will be attending. "What's your schedule like? Let's do it *now.*"

As he accompanies her downstairs to her office, John Wood asks, "Was that Allan Gilmour on the phone? What did he say?" She explains it was her father-in-law, calling to say that the baby's temperature was down. "She has the flu." John Wood makes no comment, expresses no interest.

Nancy Badore stops in the reception room to get a bowl of sliced fruit. "I need *fuel.* Healthy fuel!" She and John Wood enter her office, where Mary Aughton and Janice Turowski are waiting at the round worktable. The purpose of this meeting is to go over the logistics of the Senior Executive Program for August, which will be held in London instead of Detroit. The EDC does occasional "road shows" in order to demonstrate its international scope. Janice Turowski and Mary Aughton oversee administrative details—who will be attending the meeting, hotel, meals, travel arrangements.

"I wanted this meeting so I don't go into things in my usual dream state," jokes Nancy Badore as she sits down. "Also, I want to make one thing clear: *I'm* the one who gets the honeymoon suite in the hotel, because I'm the one who's traveling with a nanny and a baby!" She laughs.

The three continue to brief her on trip and seminar details. There is talk about difficulties dealing with one of the men at the hotel. Nancy Badore advises Janice Turowski, "I'm sure you can work it out with him, but you're going to have to keep your confidence high when you do it!" The advice is similar to that she gave Al Solvay when he was having trouble with the seminar teacher: work it out, I have confidence in you. Later she explains, "When people are at loggerheads, sometimes they just need encouragement to keep going. I try to show people that I have every confidence in them—that can often help turn a situation around. This is especially true with women. I find it often takes women ten years longer than men to realize how good they really are. I don't think you can make a contribution until you've moved *beyond* wondering if you're good enough. So I try to give them opportunities to discover that, occasions to build their confidence."

Mary Aughton says she thinks they should invite the London participants' wives to a luncheon. "I need to start a file on this trip," says Nancy Badore. She takes graph paper from her desk, begins jotting notes. "I can see I should begin thinking about my welcoming speech."

As the meeting ends, she calls in Dee Durocher and hands her the task list. "I'm starting a file on London—this goes in it." Then she stands up. "Thank you all for coming. You've made me feel more like this trip is a reality. We *are* going to London. We *will* have a terrific time! There's been so much to do, I haven't focused on it."

Janice Turowski, Mary Aughton, and John Wood leave the office at just after 1:00. A phone call comes in from the author to whom Nancy Badore dictated a letter this morning. She greets him in a friendly voice, but is very direct. "The main problem is that half the quotes you attributed to me are totally wrong!" She stands as she talks, speaking forcefully, but also laughing on occasion. "I sent you a list of people you should be talking to on this. Of course, we'll be in touch."

Hanging up, she asks Dee Durocher to call out for a tuna salad, then glances briefly at the large television monitor in her office. It is on all the time: now NASDAQ index figures dance by. Beneath the monitor, sits a gym-quality rowing machine. "I use the machine whenever I have a bunch of tapes I have to watch. Usually during the lunch hour or at the end of a day. I just put the tapes on and start rowing. It was only after the baby that I started regular exercise." She also has two exercise instructors who come in two days a week at noon to put her through the paces.

"They provide the structure. That's what I need. I'm no good at providing it myself. This has been a big discovery for me—that I have to organize for structure, and that often means getting other people to provide it. One of the great things I've been doing lately is learning to face what I am *not* good at—to accept it, and then deal with it instead of pretending it will go away. So now I surround myself with people who are good at organizing *me,* and I have time for a lot more—even exercise!"

At 1:30 Nancy Badore's tuna salad arrives in a plastic carryout case. Dee Durocher enters her office with a stack of mail. Every other day, they schedule an hour to go over the mail together, in order to keep it from piling up—another example of Nancy Badore using someone else to provide her with structure. "You read while I chew," she says to Dee Durocher, who sits down and piles three folders in neat stacks. Today's mail comprises about twenty pieces. Dee Durocher begins handing it to Nancy Badore. The first item is a thank-you from Anheuser-Busch; a group of its executives recently visited EDC. Next is a clipsheet of all the industry news for the day, with items of special interest marked in yellow highlight. Nancy Badore skims it, then sets it aside for a thorough reading later on.

There is a memo about a speech she is giving the following week. "Let's start a fact sheet on this, Dee. Some things I need to know: the size of the room. The

layout. The size of the audience. The seating arrangement." Nancy Badore gives many speeches, both within
Ford and to other industry and management groups. She
writes all her own material, usually at the last moment,
after working out her ideas by talking them through,
getting most of her inspiration "from verbal exchange."
But despite this seat-of-the-pants way of working, she
likes to be very deliberate in terms of having all the
background information. Again, she relies on Dee Durocher to provide her with structure—in this case, facts
that will help her organize herself for the speech.

Dee Durocher hands her a message slip. "This woman
says you told her to call about having lunch. So I scheduled it for August 2."

"I have no idea who she is," says Nancy Badore,
reading the name. "But I guess I'll find out." She decides the caller is probably the daughter of one of Ford's
executives; she makes a habit of taking daughters to
lunch to give them advice. "As soon as these men's
daughters become interested in careers, you find the
fathers' attitudes toward women in business really
change. So I try to encourage them all I can." In addition to counseling managers' daughters, she also gives
advice to freshmen women entering Ford. "I used to
have an open-door policy for all the women in the company, but I found I was spending too much time, and
always dealing with things on a crisis basis. So I tried to
get organized and be more proactive. Now I ask the
young women coming in to set up their own network

groups—I go and speak to them, give advice, but they do the organization. It's really gotten a network going around here."

The next item is an expense voucher from one of her direct reports. "What's this item?" she asks Dee Durocher as she studies it.

"Oh, that's for a class he signed up for, then canceled out of because you called a meeting," Dee explains.

"He canceled a *class* because I called a *meeting?*" Nancy Badore shakes her head. "Okay, Dee, I need to dictate. Write this: 'I am signing your voucher for the cost of the class you canceled but'—now I want this in caps—'BUT WHEN ARE YOU GOING TO DO SOMETHING FOR YOURSELF? WHEN ARE YOU GOING TO BELIEVE IN YOUR OWN DEVELOPMENT? Best, Nancy. P.S. WHEN IS YOUR NEXT CLASS?' "

Dee Durocher goes over some new appointments she has scheduled during the coming weeks. "Dee does my schedule and keeps my appointment book, filling it for the next three months. I have it with me only when I'm traveling. It's convenient this way, but we're both looking for another system. While this is efficient, I'm not sure it's best—we're both trying to find a way I can initiate more of my schedule, instead of reacting passively, having my time filled. I'm not sure how I can do that and not waste a lot of time, but we'll find a way."

There are more thank you letters—for speeches given, favors done; then a nomination for an award: "How nice!" Nancy Badore glances over a list showing recent promotions within the company. "Great! I see we're getting *people* people in these jobs!"

At 2:45 Dee Durocher finishes the mail. "Tell Antigone I'm ready," says Nancy Badore, and Antigone Kiriacopoulou comes in. She is a consultant who helps design programs for the EDC; she and Nancy Badore worked together with Employee Involvement programs for six years before the EDC was started.

Antigone asks if she can shut the door, then she sits down at the worktable. Closeted together, the two women have a slight air of coconspirators. Briefly, they discuss Antigone's new baby. Nancy Badore mentions Maggie's cold. Then it's on to the substance of the meeting.

Antigone worked on the Japanese Business Associations—the EDC's program on doing business with the Japanese. It has been one of the most successful programs, and now the EDC must transfer it to another school within Ford that serves more than just the top layer of the management pyramid. The transition is delicate, and Nancy Badore and Antigone discuss the various personalities involved to try to decide who might best handle it, how to avoid stepping on toes. "And we've got to do it all without reducing the quality of the program," says Nancy Badore.

"Plus we've got to move on to the *Korean* Business Associations," says Antigone. "Dick and I are surveying the population [of Ford's managers] to see who can best benefit."

They discuss which interns might be used in managing the transfer. "We need to find how these different tasks can tap into *their* career aspirations," says Nancy Badore. She gets up, moves around a bit, seeming restless. Opening her handbag, she puts on lipstick.

Antigone observes that they must figure a way to redesign the Japanese program that is being retained, so they can connect to the program being transferred.

"So what do we do now?" asks Nancy Badore. "I think a practical start would be for me to host a meeting on the transfer. Get everything out in the open, bring in all the people involved."

At 3:15 Antigone closes her notebook. "I'm really sorry, but I have to run."

"Oh, sure, sure. I know this meeting started late."

As Antigone leaves, Nancy Badore gets up and stretches. "I've been sitting for hours. I need to get up and move around!"

She walks quickly from her office, and begins strolling around the center, entering offices, asking people how they're doing. She stops to ask John Walker what time he wants to come by for the brief meeting they need to have. They decide on 4:15, then she moves on, visiting with her program directors briefly, mostly joking—these visits are just to keep in touch. She makes her way back to the cramped quarters where the administration staff is housed, grousing about the architectural layout she inherited. "For what's supposed to be an egalitarian operation, our respective offices go from Versailles to monks' cells in record time," she says in disgust. Then she walks upstairs to the meeting rooms where the managers in the Senior Executive Program are on view behind glass walls of the meeting rooms.

Again she mentions the importance of breakouts in these sessions. "So often programs of this type are overstructured, as if people can't be trusted to use free time well. But what these guys need is a chance to sit around and talk among themselves—complain, praise, and think about what is being said in the sessions. We want them to ask themselves questions like, do I buy what's going on here? Is it helpful to what I'm doing? Does it address my problems? We want to get them in a challenging mode, because that gets them communicating across barriers."

She explains that the EDC tries also to get the top Ford officers who address the classes to work in a different way, to challenge themselves. "For example, we don't let the officers use speechwriters. They are asked to speak from their own notes. The officers turned out to be most effective that way, although you can imagine how much resistance we had on that one from their staff people!"

The purpose, says Nancy Badore, is to encourage candor. "Candor is incredibly dynamic in a corporation. What we've discovered is that a person, a speaker, doesn't have to be dynamic in and of himself; if he's speaking *candidly,* that dynamism will come through. Our challenge is to get the officers who come in here to share with these guys whatever they feel *passionately* about. Sometimes we interview senior people in front of a class to start off the session, and we ask them very blunt questions. Have you ever thought of leaving the company? Why? Who was the worst boss you ever had? What made him bad?" Nancy Badore stops at the food table, picks up a muffin, begins munching as she walks around and talks, gesturing, animated. "You have to ask the right questions if you want to loosen up that pyramid. Do a little teasing, bring out the humor. There has to be humor and compassion in a company these days, and we work to bring that out. This muffin is absolutely horrible!"

A group of men is filing from a classroom into a breakout session. Nancy Badore nods approvingly. "During their sessions here, we ask the managers to comment—say what they like about trends in the company, and what they worry about. We have them put it in a newsletter. The format is, 'Here's the good news, and here's the bad news.' No problem is too small for the bad news—it's those little niggling problems that eat away at people's morale."

She returns to her office, after grabbing another diet Coke. It is now 3:50. She has spent thirty-five minutes walking around, taking the center's pulse. Now she spends twenty minutes returning six of the phone calls that came in during her three-and-a-half-hour morning meeting.

At 4:15 John Walker comes in. He hands her a memo about a meeting the following morning regarding cooperation between various programs in different Ford schools. Nancy Badore reads it through. "I'm not impressed by this memo. So full of jargon."

John Walker agrees. "I thought it was *awful.*"

She takes her shoes off, puts her feet on a chair, snaps open her diet Coke, then passes the memo back. He reads it aloud, mocking the language, the training professions' gobbledygook. She laughs, but says, "I do think you should go. I can't, and I think we should be represented."

He objects. "This meeting will be a waste of time. And this memo!"

"But this is something we have to be involved in. Let me put it this way, John: I *invite* you to go. But feel free to leave at any time. If you were Bush, and Gorby and Thatcher were having a meeting, would you decide not to go because you didn't like the memo?"

He agrees. They move on to the topic of what his function will be at EDC. She says, "Me, or whoever sits in this chair after me—our job is to be crazy. To think up wild things, without censoring them. To come up with ideas fast even if they seem incongruous. I need the person who sits in your chair to provide the balance, be the sane one; inject logic and caution into the process." She thinks for a moment, then expands her definition of

172

the difference between what she calls crazy and what she calls sane. "You could define it this way: it's the difference between *divergent* and *convergent* thinking, divergent being the exploding mind that embraces the plausible *and* the implausible; convergent being the logical mind that hooks things together."

At 4:40 John Walker leaves, still voicing objections to tomorrow's meeting. She suggests that he think up something to bring up that will make the meeting more interesting. Then she goes to her desk and returns three more calls. As she shuffles through the items of mail she earlier put aside for reading—the clipsheet, an industry newsletter, she talks about how important taking the Myers-Briggs Type Indicator, a personality test, was to her in developing her own managerial style. "It showed me, very plainly in black and white, exactly where my strengths and weaknesses lie, and that has been invaluable. For instance, what I've been saying about structure, and how I need to surround myself with people who are good at providing it because I'm not—I recognized that weakness from the test. Also, I saw that one thing I'm not good at is *closure*—I get very involved in what's happening at the time, and am not good at cutting it off. Recognizing these weaknesses has been so helpful to me! Instead of pretending they'll go away, I realize that they are basic parts of who I am; they need to be worked on constantly, and must always be taken into account. It's a much more realistic approach."

She returns four more phone calls, spending a few

minutes on each. Then John Walker stops in to tell her that he has taken her advice, and thought up a few things to cover at tomorrow's meeting. "That's great, John! Now I really know it can be of some value."

When he leaves, she returns to talking about the Myer-Briggs test. I ask her how she became so enthusiastic about it.

"It happened a number of years ago. I was designing a program, and having a very hard time working with this other woman, my first subordinate. We just did *not* get along—we didn't even understand what the other was talking about. Here our business was getting people to communicate, and *we* couldn't. Then a consultant came in to work with our group, and she saw right off this woman and I were having trouble. She suggested that we take the test. It turned out we were *total* opposites in every category of the personality profile. No wonder we didn't understand one another! But after getting feedback on our differences, we began to work with those differences in mind; I put myself in her position, tried to see how she would respond to something, based on the information I had about who she was. She did the same, and we began to get along beautifully.

"But it was more than that. My chance encounter with this test really enabled me to find my *voice*. I realized why I had never really fitted in. Here I was working with all these technical, thinking types, yet I was intuitive and extroverted, getting my ideas quickly and stimulated by contact with people. Plus, I had spent all this time in

174

academia, writing and getting my Ph.D., and what I really liked most was to talk! I began to realize that I'd spent a lot of time trying fruitlessly to fit in, be like everyone else—and that I had been prepared to spend the rest of my life doing so. But the test gave me confirmation that I had qualities that could be of value in a company like this. I had something special to contribute, but *only* if I could be myself. So I began glorying in who I was, instead of trying to suppress it. And ever since then, I've not only been more effective, I've also had a great time here at Ford. I don't have to labor under the strain that comes from repression."

It is 6:00. Nancy Badore gets up and begins tidying her office, clearing off the desk, preparing for tomorrow morning. She says she used to work until at least 7:00, but since having the baby she leaves at around 6:00. She drives home to Dearborn in "one of the new cars they give us to evaluate every few months," using her time in the car just to think. "I'm very conscious of letting my brain wander and float while I'm driving. I don't turn the radio on, I don't concentrate on tasks I have to do. The day's so fast-paced, it's hard to find time to totally tune out; I do that in the car, and find I have some of my most creative moments while driving on the highway." Not inappropriate for one who has made her career at Ford.

CHAPTER SEVEN

The Leader as Transmitter:

Dorothy Brunson,
Brunson Communications

D orothy Brunson has a strong image of herself as "a transmitter"—gathering information from everywhere, making sense of it, rearranging it in patterns, and then beaming it out to wherever it needs to go. She compares herself to one of the big radio towers that she owns. But it's more than just a metaphor or image; it's also an apt description of Dorothy Brunson's highly evolved and conscious leadership style, which derives from the constant need to monitor and absorb new information in order to keep up in a business where the only constant is change—"to survive, you have to anticipate your changing audience." To this end, Dorothy Brunson has learned to adapt her forceful and very direct persona to whatever the occasion demands, switching roles with great facility and a sense of gusto and enjoyment, always eliciting and transmitting as much information as possible.

Dorothy Brunson is owner and president of Brunson Communications, which owns three radio stations in Baltimore, Atlanta, and Wilmington, North Carolina. With

179

the recent acquisition of an FCC license for a television station in Philadelphia, her company will be worth approximately $15 million.

At fifty-two years old, she is considered one of contemporary radio's pioneers, a "Revolutionary of Radio," as she has been called. During the seventies, as general manager of and corporate general manager of Inner City Broadcasting Corporation, then the nation's largest black-owned radio network, she developed the now-ubiquitous "urban contemporary" format, a blend of black and white music for sophisticated big city markets that crossed racial lines. She also pioneered the influential black community based call-in and talk format for AM radio.

Dorothy Brunson got her start in radio in 1964, with Sonderling Broadcasting Corporation, as assistant controller of station WWRL in New York City. She soon moved on to chief controller, then assistant general manager, finally serving as liaison between WWRL and the parent company. In 1973, she was named general manager of WLIB, a black-audience station that at the time was failing badly. After she aided in the purchase of the FM station WBLS, and redesigned the format, the FM became the nation's sixth largest billing station, black or white, and was number one in total audience listenership for five straight years.

In 1979, at the top of her field, she decided to leave her successful career and look for a radio station that could become the base of her own broadcasting network. With her background in the financial aspect of the business—planning, accounting, and bookkeeping—as well as the working relationships she had established with several banks, she managed to raise $500,000 in venture capital and was extended a $2 million credit line. A director of a venture capital firm that backed her explained that they invested in Dorothy Brunson "not because she was a woman or because she was black," but because she was that rarity in broadcasting, someone "who really understood cash flow."

A bankruptcy judge accepted Dorothy Brunson's bid of $530,000 for station WEBB in Baltimore, a station in such bad financial shape that its water and telephone had been turned off, its ceiling had caved in, and creditors had repossessed its feeble transmitter. Brunson moved from New York to Baltimore with her two sons (she and her husband had divorced in the mid-seventies), and began the task of restoring the station to respectability and $2 million a year profitability. While doing so, she bought her two other radio stations, engaged in a four-year battle to acquire the television license, and—ever the entrepreneur—joined with several partners to start a food service company that operates in airports, aquariums, convention centers, and large off-premises public facilities.

Dorothy Brunson runs her business out of her Baltimore station, WEBB, where she also serves as general manager. At 8:15 on a June morning, she arrives, carrying a tub of 7-Eleven coffee. "I made the mistake of stopping to pick up this coffee, and whenever I stop, I run into someone and start gabbing." She passes the Maryland office of Congressman Kweisi Mfume on the first floor of her two-story red brick building, then climbs the stairs to where she has her offices. The bright, airy reception room features an eclectic mix of signed Romare Bearden prints and miscellaneous photos of Africans.

Dorothy Brunson is a woman built on a large scale, but not fat, with a slight Indian cast to her features. Today, wearing a plain black cotton dress and department-store earrings, she is completely unpretentious. At the outer desk, she picks up three messages and greets the receptionist: "Good morning, Ms. Joyce!" No one in Dorothy Brunson's company is called by his or her first name.

She explains why: "This is a black organization, so it's common for people to have a strong need for self-esteem. In that situation, a pecking order can develop. In this business, there tends to be a pecking order anyway—the sales manager is more important than the salesman, that sort of thing. I find when you call everyone either Mr. or Ms., it works as a great equalizer, and the tendency to establish a pecking order is diminished. So you'll end up with an account executive going to get coffee, *or* the janitor, but it doesn't seem demeaning because they all have the feeling that they're important.

I really think a lot of businesses underestimate the need people have to feel important in their jobs—sure they want to make money and be happy, but they also want to feel as if they're somebody. Calling a young guy "Mr." for the first time in his life makes him feel that way. He acts up to the way you address him. Plus it cuts down on my need to hand out a lot of titles and give useless promotions as a stroke. And that saves my stations money."

Passing down the hall, Dorothy Brunson greets her staff with amused good humor. To the controller she calls, "Good morning, Mr. Walls! I hope you're not going to keep me too busy today." In the big center conference room with its open spaces and glass walls, she kicks off two-inch heels and puts on broken-in flats, then enters the smaller of her two adjoining offices at the rear of the building. She sets down her tub of coffee. "This is where I play general manager," she says. "When I'm in here, I'm not such a big shot. I don't do anything corporate in this room—it doesn't feel right."

Although the morning gospel show being done in the studio down the hall is piped softly into all the offices, Dorothy Brunson also switches on the small plastic boom box on the windowsill by the desk. "I listen to radio all day long, from the time I get up. I monitor what we're doing here, and spend time listening to the competition. I have a policy: everyone who works here has to spend two days a week listening to other stations, then report to me on what's going on. A lot of big radio networks have sophisticated monitoring equipment. *I* do everything by listening and by gut."

With the radio on, she glances briefly at the mail piled on her desk. It's in disarray because her secretary has been out all week. She hasn't hired a temporary because "I wouldn't know where to tell her to find stuff." As a result, she has been answering her mail at home at night.

"My secretary goes through the mail as soon as it comes in and throws out what I call the smut. The really pointless junk—she's been with me a long time, so she decides. She usually has it done by about ten, and she brings it in to me. I see everything after that."

If the letter demands her response, Dorothy Brunson will attend to it on the spot. "I have all these form letters made up to cover almost every contingency, so I'll return the letter to Brenda with the number of the form to use. But I'll always include an extra line or two—I write it right in the margins—so it will be a personal response. But with most of my mail, I route it. I decide who should see it and what they should do about it. I make a suggestion, scribble it on the letter, date it, and send it on. There's an unwritten rule in my company that you have to get back to me with your response within three days."

Dorothy Brunson believes mail is very important—so important that, when she visits her different stations, she will often ask her general manager to sit down and show her exactly how he or she does the mail. "I use it as a way of training. I show them how they can get more out

184

of their mail. For example, I might see them about to toss out a notice about some community organization that's having a flea market or sponsoring a little parade. I'll see an angle—maybe we can send an MC to host the event and do some kind of promotion. There's usually *something* we can do. I give them ideas, stimulate their imaginations. Teach them that mail isn't just a chore to be gotten through. It's something that *connects* them to what's going on."

Now, in her smaller office, Dorothy Brunson picks up the phone and dials a disc jockey at a competitor's station, with whom she spoke briefly yesterday.

"Michael? Well, I'm sorry to interrupt your shower. I thought you might be interested in talking about opportunity." She reaches into her old black handbag, pulls out a sloppy plastic-bound daybook filled with notes, cards, slips of paper. She finds the page for the day, glances over it. "How about today? What's your schedule? Around three?"

Hanging up, she notes the appointment. She often spends the first half hour of her day adding more appointments to those already scheduled. She likes to do that, and her days are structured to allow for plenty of flexibility, so she can follow up on new information—picking up signals in her transmitter mode.

Today's first meeting, scheduled for 9:00, is with the local representative for the Department of Housing and Urban Development. HUD is a large client of station WEBB, advertising the hundreds of houses it repos-

185

sesses. This morning, Dorothy Brunson has invited the HUD representative to her office to meet another of her clients, who runs a local stress clinic. "I'm sort of a matchmaker on this one—trying to bring two clients together so they'll both love me more."

She hasn't sat down yet. Standing, sipping coffee, she telephones her national sales representative in New York. In radio, a national rep's job is to expand the pool of advertisers. Dorothy Brunson asks the agent right off about Sears, a longtime advertiser on her stations. The company's new every-day-is-a-sale-day policy means a big cutback on its sale ads.

As the rep talks, Dorothy Brunson pulls out a pad of paper and jots down figures. She doesn't sound very happy. "You're not *telling* me anything," she complains. She informs the rep that her national sales manager from Atlanta will be in New York next week. "He's going to be involved in this every step of the way." The rep objects. "Well, I'm sorry if you don't like it, you haven't sent a good act down here to us in years." She laughs good-naturedly and, as she hangs up, laughs again. "Don't you send me love. Send money!"

"Dealt with *him*," is her comment, as she searches her handbag for her glasses. She smiles in a satisfied way. "You've got to have a little different technique with everyone you talk to. With some, you're diplomatic, some you tease, some you joke around with. The trick is to get what *you* want, but keep them happy too, so they'll want to keep doing business with you." She says she's good at knowing how to keep people happy because she studies their personalities. "It's one of the most important things you can do in business. I'm constantly ingesting information about people into my head. I watch how they move, how they dress. Are they neat or sloppy? I try to see what their desk drawers look like. Are they always in need of money? How do they talk to a secretary on the phone? Do they get upset easily? The more you know about someone, the better position you put yourself in to know how to handle him, how to get him to respond to what you want."

It is now just after 9:00. She buzzes the receptionist and finds that Mr. Cross, the man from HUD, has not arrived. She dials his office. "Well, at least he's left. That's a good sign." But she calls the stress clinic client she wants him to meet with and tells her to hold off on coming over until he arrives. "No telling with him." Then she explains. "See, that's what I mean. This guy's schedule usually leans toward late. Since he's a client, not my employee, that's not for me to judge about him. But it helps me to know that about him."

She buzzes the reception desk again, and tells the young woman to please send Vashti McKenzie in to see her. They might as well use the time they're waiting for Mr. Cross to have their meeting. For her meeting with Vashti McKenzie, Dorothy Brunson steps into her other office. This second office has a huge desk with a high leather chair and long sofa. "In here, I'm important. This is where I do my corporate stuff."

The receptionist ushers in a tall black woman in her early thirties. Vashti McKenzie does the 6-to-9 A.M. gospel show on WEBB; she's been with the station for seven years and has become very much identified with it. But she is also the minister of the fast-growing congregation of a one hundred-year-old local church, a candidate for a doctorate in divinity, and the mother of three young children. Ten days ago, she sent Dorothy Brunson a memo requesting six weeks off—she needed more time to devote to her ministry. "She asked me very casually," says Dorothy Brunson. "So I asked her, what can be changed? She said nothing—she had nothing to negotiate. Her ministry comes first. Well, of course, that's how it should be. But now I'm left with a problem I have to solve. I've got to think of what's good for the station."

Dorothy Brunson directs Vashti McKenzie to sit beside her on the sofa in her office. She places the container of coffee on the floor. "Vashti, we've got a problem," she says, making the young woman the sole exception to her habit of calling people in the office "Mr." or "Ms." Later, she explains the reason: "Vashti is a minister. People call her Reverend. Usually, that's what I call her—Rev. But this was such a delicate sort of conversation, about her future at the station. I could hardly sit there on the couch with her and call her Reverend."

They begin by discussing possibilities for Vashti's replacement. The other disc jockeys at WEBB are mostly young men who do the urban contemporary programming that Dorothy Brunson pioneered in New York. "We can't just pull someone in to do gospel," says Dorothy Brunson. She plays with her glasses as she talks. "They've got to have credibility in the community. And there is no one like that who would be willing to take a job on a provisional basis, for just six weeks. We're looking at something here that's going to be leading into *the whole day*. If we don't do it right, we could disappear down a hole."

Dorothy Brunson reminds Vashti of the time four years ago when she took off a month to have her third child. "Of course you had to do it, but the morning ratings when you were gone almost killed us! It took years to rebuild. And we're in a more delicate situation now, with a twenty-four hour gospel station on the air. We lose listeners, we may never get them back." Dorothy Brunson wonders how much longer Vashti will be able to do the program at all. "I've talked to a number of people who've had experience with your new bishop. He's very well trained and well read—and *ambitious*. He's going to be using you more and more. I don't see this problem as going away." Dorothy Brunson points out that Vashti's congregation has grown quickly since she took over as pastor. "To be honest, I don't know how much longer you can keep doing this show five mornings a week."

So Vashti's request must be considered in a larger context: maybe this is the time she should leave the morning slot for good. "I'll be interviewing a young man this afternoon," says Dorothy Brunson. "I don't know what I'm going to do. I just wanted to share with you that I'm looking at a lot of possibilities."

They talk at some length about Vashti's church, the various missions that have been started, then in a general way about radio, how the audience for gospel is changing. Now Dorothy Brunson's role becomes more that of mentor than decision-maker or boss. She listens intently to Vashti's assessments, nodding her head, encouraging. "You're right. I understand." She laughs a lot, and her Georgia accent comes through—though raised in New York, she was born in Georgia and retains that air. The feeling in the room, the easy attitude toward talk and time, takes on the front-porch flavor of the rural South.

It's just after 10:30 when Dorothy Brunson begins to wrap up the meeting, switching from general topics to the specific future. "Well, I'm at a crossroads. I don't know *what* direction I'll choose. But I'll know tomorrow afternoon, and you'll be the first to hear my decision."

Vashti asks, "What are you really looking for?"

"I'm not sure."

"Well, let's pray on it."

"That's been done."

Dorothy Brunson walks Vashti into the glass-walled conference room. After saying goodbye, she explains, "I mean it when I say that I haven't decided yet. I'm going to be spending today and tomorrow gathering all

190

the information I can, all the data. I'll decide based on that. That's how I always work."

What data? What information? "Well, of course I started with the ratings service data. I analyze that all the time, both to see how we're doing at the moment and what sort of trends emerge over time. In Vashti's case, each of the last three ratings books showed a decline in morning listenership. The all-gospel station kept picking up our listeners, especially the core group of women between twenty-five and fifty-four. No matter how we counterprogrammed, the erosion continued. I was concerned and Vashti knew it—I am very direct—so she had that information when she asked for this leave. Now I've reached a point of action: the time to make a change is always during the summer, because the most important ratings books are done in the fall.

"Anyway, that's the background of the process. I've been monitoring Vashti's show for months. In radio, you monitor all your employees, on and off air, because they must constantly generate audience listenership. The more people they are able to attract, the more money we can make off their show and the more popular they become. In any business, people must have an ability to respond to change, but in radio that's especially true. So you have to keep examining your people, see if they're in the right rhythm, if they're working well with their peers, if their commitment is high, if they keep pushing that extra bit, coming up with new ideas."

Dorothy Brunson explains that she dismisses people

all the time; again, that's the nature of radio. "But I dismiss in a constructive way. When I fire you, I'll be very direct, tell you just where the problem lies. Maybe it's *not* with you, maybe the market has changed. But if you *do* have a problem, you'll know it. And I'll tell you what are your strengths and what are your weaknesses, based upon my close observation and my experience. With employees, I notice everything. Is a person always waiting on payday for his check? That's a sure sign he isn't managing his money. Maybe I'll sit down with you and help you clean one of your desk drawers—I'll show you how your paperwork is careless, or that you have a tendency to hoard things, and make it clear how that got in your way. Years later, I've had people come to me and thank me for firing them. They say they learn a lot from the experience!"

Dorothy Brunson opens the door from the conference room and says to the receptionist, "Ms. Joyce, will you please call Mr. Cross's office and inform his secretary that he was due here at nine!"

Back in her corporate office, she sits down to take a call, and her tone switches from front-porch Georgia to back-room Texas. The caller is a banker from whom she's trying to borrow $1.5 million as a backup fund for refurbishing the television station she has bought in Philadelphia. "George! How're you doing, stranger? So, are we doing a deal or not? I don't believe you! Convince me. Cash flow in April? Everybody's profitable." From memory she reels off figures, the profits from her various enterprises. "I'll be here tomorrow if you want to get back to me on this. I know it's Saturday—what do you think, we only work five days a week around here?"

Hanging up, she explains, "One of my policies is to borrow money *before* I need it. In business, it's important to know where your dollars are coming from. That can be *the* thing that makes the difference. You can't seize an opportunity if you first have to run around scrounging for money."

It is nearing 11:00. Dorothy Brunson walks down the hall to the office of her local sales manager, a man in a well-tailored suit who wears his fraternity pin on his lapel. "Mr. Johnson! I'd like you at the meeting I'm having with Mr. Mickens this afternoon," she says, referring to her national sales manager, who has just flown in from Atlanta on his way to New York. "We need to talk a little strategy."

"Mrs. B., I can't. I've got client meetings. One at one, one at three, one at four . . ."

"All right, then. Get out there and sell. I'm not going to be the one who tells you not to make money."

Stopping in her smaller office, she turns the boom box off, and finds her coffee has grown cold. She carries the cup into the small lunchroom across from the studio and cuts off the top of the Styrofoam container so she can fit it into the microwave. Then she carries the mangled but heated cup back into her larger office. Her next hour is devoted to taking and making five telephone calls.

193

First, she calls the manager of her Atlanta station. Pulling out a white pad, she jots down the sales figures he gives her. She will use them during her afternoon meeting with Mr. Mickens.

Next, a call from her minister. "Hello, Dr. Strickland!" They discuss the need for a musician—perhaps an ad over the airwaves—and a woman in the church whose son has won a college scholarship to a major university. The family can't afford the room and board, so the church is trying to raise the money.

"I deal with these things on different levels," Dorothy Brunson explains after she and the minister have talked, expanding on her view of herself as a transmitter adapting various roles in order to elicit more information. "I do grass-roots work at my church as director of adult education. But I also sit on boards that are very powerful, so I'm able to translate needs at both levels— identifying a need a young person might have for education, say, in this instance, then finding a way to supply those needs. You've got a lot of people on boards who don't have that grass-roots touch. They do charity fund-raisers, but they don't know what it's like for people who are trying to raise a family on $30,000 a year. Working both ends—that takes being able to operate on all the different levels, play different roles. But that's what I like doing."

Mr. Cross, the man from HUD, returns the call she made to remind him of their meeting. "Well, where've *you* been? I was expecting you in here at nine!" He tries to change the date for their meeting to the following week. "Monday?" she says. "Why not today? Why not drop in here at around four?"

She buzzes the receptionist, tells her to call Ms. Pulliam, the client she is trying to put together with Mr. Cross. "Tell her the meeting's at four, but not to come until someone calls and tells her he's actually being seated!" Why isn't Dorothy Brunson more annoyed at Mr. Cross's failure to show up for a scheduled appointment? "He's a *client*. How am I going to object?"

Another call comes in. "Reverend Wade! Good morning, sir. Well, if you hadn't been there, I would have come looking for you. No, I've got these two pistols I keep here on my desk." She laughs as if enjoying a tremendous joke, playing a role as she stands behind her big desk. "I know," she says, "I'm aware that people from here have been calling you. But it was all your fault, you weren't giving me my money! Of course, I didn't want to cut you off. I like doing business with you. But you forced my hand."

She listens, nodding and chuckling. "That's all right, I brought my bodyguards with me, I was safe. Sure, we're still in a position where we can do business."

Hanging up, she explains. "Every personality is different. This minister is a real jackleg sort of guy. I never come at him from a rational point of view. With him, I play the role of desperado." The minister advertises on her station, does spots to solicit donations. "Some people say, why do you let someone like him advertise? But

I don't make religious judgments about community-based or established churches. You never know what direction good is coming from. But if a church advertises on my station, it *pays*. My *own* church pays! That guy, he does very well, but doesn't want to pay. My bookkeeper kept sending him bills. Then the sales manager called him.

"When *nothing* works, I have to step in and be the heavy. But I have to do it diplomatically, and not insult the client so that he doesn't want to come back." In this particular instance, the minister asked Dorothy Brunson to meet him at midnight if she wanted her money. "Then he said, maybe coming out that late would be dangerous. Trying to scare me, you know the kind of thing. So I told him, don't you worry. I'll be there, but I'll have my bodyguards. So I showed up at midnight with my two big sons."

It is now 12:10. Mr. Walls, the controller, enters her big office. "When Mr. Walls comes in, I always end up signing checks." Dorothy Brunson signs a pile of them, then steps into her smaller office. The local sales manager stops in to ask how she thinks they can get the young people at a concert that evening to identify the station.

"Why not have *two* DJs host the show? They can talk things up." The sales manager nods, says he'll cut some promotional spots in the studio. Dorothy Brunson is left sorting through the mail piled on her desk. "I'm *drowning* in paper with my secretary away."

Exchanging flats for two-inch heels, she gathers up her purse at 12:30 and goes outside to where her son's Mazda is parked. One of her sons, a student at Morehouse College in Atlanta, is working in New York for the summer, living in a house Brunson still owns with her former husband off Riverside Drive. "I'm driving my son's car now," she says, "because I finally had to give up my old '79 Buick. I called that car Josephine." She explains that, not long ago, she was visited by a reporter from *Essence* magazine, who was doing a story on "Black Millionairesses." "I sure disappointed him with my car!" she recalls with delight. "He expected a Rolls or a Jaguar or some nonsense." She gestures to her black cotton dress. "Also, jewelry and furs. But I don't put a high value on that stuff."

She drives past the tangible assets she *does* value— three enormous radio towers on 7.7 acres of prime real estate she owns behind the station. As she drives, she switches around on the radio. "I'm always listening, always tuning in." She explains that, although she acts as general manager for WEBB, she doesn't get involved with day-to-day operations. "But with all three of my stations, I *do* get involved with clients. My role is really to make contacts, to represent my stations in the world. It's a vague sort of thing. When I do workshops, the kids always ask me, 'Mrs. B., what does the president of a company *do?*' It's a hard question. In a way, we don't do anything specific. But what we do is to knit everything together. If I'm sitting on the dais at an NAACP dinner in Atlanta, on the board of the Harlem Commonwealth Council in New York, or having dinner with some president of this or that in North Carolina, *it's all part of the same totality*. It's Dorothy Brunson working as president to keep the name of her company before the community and clients. Being out in the world, representing what you've created—that's a form of corporate development, but on a very subtle plane."

A half hour of driving through traffic and Dorothy Brunson arrives at the Forum, a one-story fieldstone building set on a wooded lot. The Forum used to be an old Jewish catering hall, but as the neighborhood changed, it began to lose business. One of the Jewish partners suggested to a black insurance agent he knew that they join together and make it a black-Jewish firm. The insurance agent, Terry Addison, asked Dorothy Brunson if she wanted to invest $60,000. She agreed to put in $20,000, and take the rest out of profits. "I'm a very active partner. I handle lots of negotiations. Our minority group of three partners has been the force behind the expansion. They'd been losing money, and now we're doing three-plus million dollars' worth of business a year." The nature of business has changed to encompass as much off-site as on-site catering. In 1987 the Forum, in conjunction with Host International, opened the Crabpot restaurant in the Baltimore airport, and now plans to expand to fifteen airports across the country. Today the three black partners are meeting over lunch to discuss a joint venture with The Marriott Corporation for the food concession at Baltimore's Harborplace National Aquarium.

Dorothy Brunson enters the building. A retirement party is going on in one of the large rooms. In another, a single table has been set up. A young man is filling water glasses. "How's it going? You learning the business?" she asks, and he nods. "Well, you'd better not mess up today, or I'll call Morgan State University to tell them to fail you in your Hotel Management courses." She smiles—now she's playing the stern but affectionate mother.

In the Forum's offices, she finds the group from Marriott—two managers and a female lawyer—with the Forum's manager, an enormous black man in red suspenders. Also Terry Addison, the partner who brought her in. "Hello, Mr. Wortherly," Dorothy Brunson greets the manager.

He introduces her around the office. "Mrs. Brunson is with us. She owns several radio stations and a TV station. And she's been on the cover of *The Wall Street Journal*, et cetera."

"Oh, you just forget about all that!"

A secretary comes in. Mrs. Brunson has a call from her controller.

"See, I can't go anywhere without someone wanting something."

Another secretary brings in a Federal Express envelope, hands it to Dorothy Brunson. As she takes the phone, she opens the envelope, which contains contracts from the Forum's Washington, D.C., offices. After answering Mr. Walls' question about a payment, she enters the room where lunch is being served.

The men from Marriott are very polite but rather strained, and an awkward moment comes when the young waiter spills iced tea on the Marriott lawyer's white dress. As he wretchedly goes to get a mop, Dorothy Brunson says, "That poor young man! He takes his job so seriously. He's going to be miserable all day."

The atmosphere becomes less strained when Brunson and Terry Addison's partner arrives. Ray Haysbert is the president of Parks Sausage Company, the first minority-owned business traded on the New York Stock Exchange. With his height, his age (nearly seventy), his legendary success, and his cagey Southern-gentleman manner, Ray Haysbert is a difficult person to condescend to, and this seems to put the Marriott people at ease. But Ray Haysbert does not do the talking; Dorothy Brunson does.

She begins by asking very detailed questions that take up a good half hour of the meeting. She wants to know about Marriott's structure, the various divisions, where the food service division fits in. She shows particular interest in the details of the company's turnpike franchises, supplementing her questions with observations about food services on various toll plazas on highways that she's traveled. She seems to be storing up information about how Marriott is run, though she doesn't take any notes. She wants the big picture, also the details. She wants to know how people are trained, how the franchising works.

Finally, as the seafood pasta course is cleared, the representative from Marriott says, "Now, give us an idea of what you do."

"Well, I'm the chairman, and Ray's the president," says Dorothy Brunson. "So I'll let Ray tell you about us."

Ray Haysbert says, "Dorothy, you keep on talking."

She describes the partnership, how it was formed, and emphasizes the *multi*ethnic aspect. "We never push the minority business thing. We do *everything*—we've got the capacity for kosher, or any type of ethnic food. That's part of why we've been so successful." She emphasizes that the partners sit on "a number of boards around town that allow them to have influence in many areas. So people know us, and we get a lot of business." Ray Haysbert adds in his understated Southern way, "We *do* know a couple of people in this city." Then he laughs. It would be hard to find a Maryland businessman with better political connections.

There follows a long discussion of a conflict with another concessionaire, who is trying to get the contract on the aquarium. There are doubts whether this other man has the legal right. "If this gets resolved," says the man from Marriott, "and we have the go-ahead, we're definitely interested in going in with you on this joint venture."

Dorothy Brunson mentions that the Forum is also interested in programs for training staff, developing young people with skills to staff the various ventures. "We're not just talking about the aquarium here, we see lots of other opportunities." Once again, she mentions the Crabpot, the Forum's chain of new airport restaurants. "We can learn from you," she says. "In twenty years, *we* want to be Marriott!"

The Marriott representative says their usual split on joint ventures is 80/20. Terry Addison seems prepared to haggle over this figure. But Dorothy Brunson says quickly that it's agreeable so long as provision is made for more favorable terms if the Forum brings in something extra on a deal.

As the meeting ends, Ray Haysbert says he "has to get back and make a few sausages." Dorothy Brunson whispers, "That's how Ray likes to talk. He's worth about twenty million dollars." Everyone steps outside. As Terry Addison gets into his Jaguar, and Ray Haysbert into his black Cadillac, there is teasing about Dorothy Brunson's old Escort. "The difference," she calls out to Terry Addison, "is that I own this one and the bank owns yours."

She is back at station WEBB at 3:15. The disc jockey she talked to first thing this morning is in the conference room outside her big office. She asks him to wait, then goes into her smaller office, where the local sales manager wants her to look over a new print ad for her three stations that reads "Congratulations! You're about to have triplets!" She calls in her national sales manager from Atlanta. "Mr. Mickens, you get in on this too. Now, what do you think? I told the ad people, think of things that come in threes." The idea is to advertise Brunson Communications' three stations as a package.

Mr. Mickens says, "I kind of like this one, Mrs. B."

"Well, we'll consider it then."

She heads into the larger office, calls in Michael, the disc jockey she's interviewing about taking over Vashti's show. "I've been listening to your programs. Both the gospel and the oldies show. Seems to me you've got a split personality." She wants to know what else he does. What does he like doing best? He mentions a program he hosts for children. "Oh? What kind of stuff? How do you deal with the children?"

They talk for a while about what makes children learn. Then Dorothy Brunson says, "Let me be frank about what's happening here." She describes the history of Vashti's morning gospel show, tells of her recent request for a leave of absence. "When she gave me the memo, I recalled the period of her pregnancy, how this station died during her time slot. So now I'm looking at the problem from various angles. I haven't decided yet— should I find a substitute, a permanent replacement, or abandon the show altogether? Move beyond gospel into something new." She tells Michael that if she continues the gospel format, she must find someone who has respect in the community. "That's very important in a town like Baltimore. Do you know, we have the highest percentage of people in church on any given Sunday of any town in this region?"

She asks him about the direction in which he sees his own life and career going. "What I'm looking for, obviously, is a fit." Then she gives him a tour of the station, shows him the studio. As she leaves him at the front door, she says, "I want you to know: I'll be making up my mind tonight. Today, I'm in the process of gathering all the information I can get. I want to be clear when I make my decision. Now, you call me if you have any questions."

She stops at the reception desk. "Has Mr. Cross called yet?" But the man from HUD has not been heard from, although it's now 4:00.

On the way back to her office, she discusses her philosophy of hiring. "I don't look for credentials so much as for people who have common *sense.* I can tell if they do by talking to them. I want to know about their lives, their goals and ambitions, what they do in their spare time, what they think about social issues, what their involvement is in the community."

To Dorothy Brunson, employees are not people from whom one buys a slice of time, and then tells what they must do in that slice. "Work has to be a commitment, not just a place to show up and earn some money. If someone thinks that way, they won't fit in around here. Work, community, your own life—these have to be tied together. If you don't bring your whole self to a problem, then you're not going to be much of a problem solver, because you're not going to be giving the best parts of your mind to thinking.

"Plus, I need people who can *think!* In radio, the market is always changing, so if you're not asking yourself what's coming next, you'll get lost. Also, if your work isn't a commitment, you're always going to be calculating what your hours are. I look for people who work whatever hours it takes to get the job done."

Passing through the conference room, she corrals her national sales manager. "Okay, it's four o'clock. Let's *talk.*"

He follows her into the big office. They each take chairs beside the big desk. It's not as cozy as the sofa on which she talked to Vashti this morning, but not as formal as if she sat behind the desk. "Now, Mr. Mickens," she begins. "You haven't given me anything from your California trip!"

He hands her a raft of papers. She studies the figures, then reads over a list of agencies and clients. "Who are these people? What do they handle?" Then, disgusted by the marketing jargon, she asks, "Do you have an English-language version of this thing?"

She mentions Mr. Mickens' recent trip to Dallas. "I want to know what you did down there." He hands her a list of Texas agencies. "This 7-Eleven thing looks promising," she says after some rapid calculation of figures.

They discuss its potential. Then she says that all her stations need better movie connections in Los Angeles.

The receptionist buzzes. The man from HUD has arrived at last. "Well, show him into the conference room." She calls out to Mr. Walls, the controller, whom she can see through the glass wall. "Please *do* something with Mr. Cross. Take him in the studio, have him cut a new ad spot. In other words, keep him busy for a bit!"

Back to the sales manager: "We need a package on this 7-Eleven thing. Call the people in Dallas, tell them we'll have something for them next week. I'll put it together." She makes a note in her loose-leaf daybook.

"Do you want to show me anything on it now?"

"With my secretary away, I can't find *anything!* Now, let's talk New York."

She warns him about the national sales rep. "Don't let him try to palm any of these minority firms off on us. I *know* all those guys. I don't need to pay a rep money to put me in touch with people I already know!"

As she's glancing over a New York agency list, Mr. Mickens brings up that he wants to give a bonus to his Atlanta assistant.

"Convince me," says Dorothy Brunson, clearly enjoying the negotiating process. "I'm open, but I want to be *convinced.*"

"She's a worker. I think she's going to exceed her goals."

After some dickering over amount, they agree on a bonus. "Mr. Mickens, you *do* love to spend money!"

A call comes in about the possibility of rain tomorrow during a promo for some furniture store. She says, "Sweeten it a little. Tell the people, they can get two albums instead of one if they come out in the rain."

The receptionist buzzes again. "Oh, Jesus! I've got to get ready for this one!" says Dorothy Brunson as she moves around behind her desk. Standing, she picks up the phone. It's a community leader from North Carolina who advertises on her station in that state.

"Hello there, Mrs. Moore! Yes, you've got a problem. And I've got a little problem too. I can't have you getting on my station and talking about another station. That's just not ethical, you know!"

The discussion turns to a rate hike Dorothy Brunson's station has recently sent the woman. "I understand, but how long have you been paying the same rate? Three *years?* Now, don't you feel a little bit ashamed? Here we've been through a recession during the last term of Ronald Reagan, and I'm still charging you the same rates!"

She listens, pulls out her white pad and starts writing. "Now, how can *I* get what I need, and still satisfy you? How about we negotiate a 25 percent increase, and I give you a month? Well, then, *you* tell *me.* Of course, I'll be glad to give you some time to save up! But I've got to get a little more. You've got to remember, the lady who owns the station has to eat too."

Her Georgia accent is coming through as she bargains. She's clearly enjoying the process. The emphasis is always on, *what can we come up with?* Finally, they agree. "Okay, I'll give you to October. Then I'll send you a memo. We can pray on it. But I'm sure we'll come to terms. You can tell by the way I talk that I don't want to lose you. We fight, but we always make up too." She hangs up. "Jesus! She mentions other stations on the air, then *I'm* supposed to carry her!"

Another call: it's Mr. Johnson, the local sales manager for the station. Dorothy Brunson tells him there's going to be a 7:30 meeting. "Yes, I'm aware tonight is Friday. Did you have something important planned?" She listens, then laughs. "Is it life or death, this meeting? That depends on how much you value your life!"

By now, Mr. Cross, the man from HUD, has cut his new ad spot, and is waiting in the big conference room beyond the glass wall. Ms. Pulliam, the client offering health services, arrives. Dorothy Brunson goes out to introduce them, giving each the political background of the other.

Both are older people, with West Indian accents. The talk has a courthouse-steps flavor. Mr. Mickens, the preppy young achiever from Atlanta, listens with a touch of impatience, then cuts in. "Mrs. B., can we wrap this up?"

"Well, Mr. Mickens, I guess you don't know who these people are," says Dorothy Brunson pointedly. "They are *clients.*" She turns to Mr. Cross and Ms. Pulliam. "I'm so glad I finally got you two together. But Mr.

Mickens here wants to get some business finished up. So why don't you two talk, and I'll be with you shortly?"

It's now after 5:00. Mr. Johnson has returned from his meetings. She asks him to drive over and get her a couple of bottles of fruit juice: "This pace is driving me to drink!" After she tells Mr. Mickens exactly what she wants from him in New York, she rejoins her clients in the glass-walled conference room, and they spend the next forty-five minutes relaxing and talking about Mayor Kurt Smolke's recent "Thank You" breakfast for his fund-raising committee, on which Dorothy Brunson served, and the various scandals overtaking HUD, which Mr. Cross serves as Baltimore director.

At 6:00 the guests leave and Dorothy Brunson returns to her larger office. Mr. Mickens is standing behind her desk. "Mr. Mickens, you don't want to sit down in that seat there! I know, you think that chair means money, wealth, and fame. But it means pain, anxiety, and a nervous stomach!"

He laughs and leaves the room. She sits down. "Here's my time to *relax!*" But she looks up to see Mr. Wortherly, the manager of the Forum, looming in her door in his red suspenders.

"I just needed three minutes of your time, Mrs. B. And I didn't know how else to get it." He opens his carrying case, brings out a stack of papers. "Here are the figures for this month."

She looks for her glasses, at first can't find them. "I'm

blind!" She locates them in the conference room. Then she looks at the figures. "These are great! This is wonderful! All this cash sitting around. I think maybe I'll have to make a motion that the directors start taking a fee." She laughs. "How about the Washington office?"

"We're still in development there."

They discuss a school in D.C. as a possible client. She asks Mr. Wortherly what he thought of today's lunch meeting with the people from Marriott. He says, "I thought it was good." She smiles. "I knew you thought that. I notice you didn't jump in when they said 20 percent. We can live with that. What's important here is the joint venture, the *long*-term deal. I would have gone for 10 percent if they'd offered it!"

Mr. Wortherly brings up the topic that is obviously on his mind, after again drawing her attention to the month's good figures. He wants a raise.

"Is that in your contract?"

"No, but since we've done so well . . ."

"So what you're saying is, the contract wasn't enough."

Again, Mr. Wortherly points out how well the company is doing.

"Here I thought we were being fair to you, but obviously I was wrong. We were being cheap and miserly and meager." Once again, Dorothy Brunson is enjoying the give-and-take of negotiation. Her desire to relax seems forgotten in the joy of testing wits with another person.

She challenges Mr. Wortherly to name a figure he believes is fair. He says he'll let *her* decide what it should be. "Now, I'm sorry, Mr. Wortherly, I can't do anything for you unless you give me a figure. In *writing.*"

"Can't I just tell you?"

"No, I want it in writing, Mr. Wortherly. Then I'll have a basis from which to negotiate. I want to be fair. I know I'm cheap, but I'm also fair."

As he leaves, she explains, "I always have people request their raises in writing. I have them spell out all the reasons they think they warrant it. They have to present me with data—we made this much more this year, and I contributed to it in these ways. By doing that, I get them thinking. They start to see their salary in context, not of what they need or want, but in terms of business—what they have contributed to profitability. This helps them focus on what they should be doing *and* teaches them to look at the bigger picture."

The controller, Mr. Walls, and Mr. Mickens now return to Dorothy Brunson's office, discussing where they will be eating tonight. She exhorts Mr. Walls—"a good family man"—to keep an eye on Mr. Mickens, a thirty-two-year-old bachelor. "I don't want all these girls in this town to find out that he's back. If they do, we've got trouble!"

The half hour between 7:00 and 7:30 dissolves as they all joke in her office, and the front-porch flavor emerges once again. Mr. Mickens—for the first time today, she calls him Vince—takes out photographs of the girl he's going to see in New York. Dorothy Brunson begins recalling his past girlfriends, comparing them, asking what happened to this one and that one, chiding him in a good-humored maternal way.

At 7:30 she goes into the lunchroom where she is holding her staff meeting. Mr. Johnson, the local sales manager, is there, looking as if he wished he were somewhere else. The young disc jockeys who work at the station trail in wearing T-shirts with slogans, turned-around baseball caps, high-top sneakers. One youth of perhaps twenty-two is wearing Bermuda shorts. "Mr. Bird! Would you do us the favor next time of wearing some pants?"

Many of the disc jockeys are also wearing large leather neck medallions in the shape of Africa. As she opens the meeting, Dorothy Brunson goes around the room, asking each what the symbolism means; all have to do with some antiapartheid message. Mr. Johnson, who's in his late thirties, points to his fraternity pin. Along with his neatly tailored suit, it seems to make a statement about the difference between his generation and the disc jockeys'.

Dorothy Brunson tells the disc jockeys that she is going to have shut-ins monitoring the stations; at the next staff meeting, she'll discuss their impressions. When several of the DJs pull out notebooks, she tells them, "You don't have to take notes. You're not here to write, you're here to *think*." She warns the DJs that they should be playing a wider range of music. "Don't exclude the females. Don't stick with too hard a sound. I listened to you, Chris. I heard your show the other night. I thought your mixes were more adult—right on the money."

Next, she explains the reason for the meeting: letting everyone know what is happening with Vashti. "I like to get everything in the open, so people don't have to wonder." She says Vashti's departure, whether temporary or permanent, is giving her a chance to rethink the station's entire format. She asks for suggestions from the staff. Should what's on now be rearranged? "We can go in a lot of different directions. How about an all-day gospel format?"

The suggestion meets with opposition, not surprisingly; few of the disc jockeys would be suited for a gospel audience. Dorothy Brunson goes around the table: "You don't like it? Tell me why." Answers are vague, except for Mr. Johnson's; he describes the potential effect on different advertisers, using data to back up his views. She addresses the disc jockeys: "Now listen to what he's saying. What I want is *specific* answers. Think about it. What do *you* think the effect would be on our markets?" Answers do grow more specific. Dorothy Brunson guides the young people in a Socratic fashion, taking her time, being patient, pushing each statement to its conclusion: "And what would *that* mean?" Her suggestion about a gospel format seems calculated to provoke thought; with a twenty-four-hour gospel station already in the Baltimore market, it seems unlikely that WEBB would consider a similar switch. But as she pursues the idea, she begins to elicit clearer thinking about what the station's mission is from her very young and very hesitant staff.

Another thing that causes her concern, she says, is the switch of two of the black stations in the area into a very adult, up-market "buppie," meaning black yuppie, sound. "That's a mix of classic jazz, classic soul, some contemporary pop. It's a direction that gives us something to think about. If we're perceived as appealing to the young, unproductive side of the market, and those other stations are aimed at the upwardly mobile, we're going to be in trouble with our advertisers."

Finishing the meeting, Dorothy Brunson says she'll be making her decision on Vashti's replacement tomorrow— a decision that will indicate the direction the station is going in. "I'll be in here all day tomorrow having a series of meetings. So anyone who thinks up anything more to say on this subject can come by and talk to me."

It's past 8:30 when the meeting adjourns. The disc jockeys hurry away. On the way out to her car, Dorothy Brunson stops to check the phone, make sure that it is locked against long distance calls. It isn't, so she fetches the key, locks it herself, then grabs up the papers she'll be reading that night in preparation for tomorrow's decision.

Dorothy Brunson made her decision the following day; as promised, Vashti was the first to know that her leave of absence meant she would have to give up her show. What she decided on, based on a resurgence in popularity of gospel, the need to define her station against a traditional all-gospel station, and the desire to appeal to a young, upwardly mobile audience, was a full show of "contemporary gospel"—crossover music done by younger artists with a pop sound, more Al Green than the Staples Singers. It's an entirely new format in radio programming, says Dorothy Brunson, "something that's never been tried before."

After making her decision, Dorothy Brunson "went to sleep. One thing I'm very good at is leaving something *alone*. In this business, you live and die by your wits, and I'm resolved not to let this job kill me. So I refuse to internalize or become anxious once I've made a decision. It's a very conscious thing, and I really had to train my mind to let things go. But it's necessary if you want to be a good boss. You can't ever set a hysterical tone, because then everybody in the company will start thrashing around, and the result will be a lot of hasty decisions. I've been a boss a long time, so I've really learned you have to transmit calm and enjoyment along with everything else."

PART III

Leadership in the New Economy

CHAPTER EIGHT

Vision and Voice

Women typically approach adulthood with the understanding that the care and empowerment of others is central to their life's work. Through listening and responding, they draw out the voices and minds of those they help to raise up. In the process, they often come to hear, value, and strengthen their own voices and minds as well.

—*Women's Ways of Knowing*
Belenky, Clinchy,
Goldberger,
and Tarule

Nothing is more common when discussing leadership today than mention of the leader's need for *vision*. Vision has become one of the buzzwords of the decade. It can be a grand-sounding way of referring to many things: a long-range plan, a particular focus, or even just the devising of a corporate slogan. In my speechwriting unit, when floundering at the top led to rampant rumors and mistrust within the company, we speechwriters were charged with printing up plastic vision cards as a way of assuring everyone that management was up to the task of imaginative leadership.

221

The authors of *Women's Ways of Knowing* explicitly contrast the metaphor of vision with that of voice. Drawing from extensive interviews, they observe that women tend to ground their descriptions of how knowledge is gained and opinions formed in terms of listening and speaking. "We found that women repeatedly used the metaphor of *voice* to depict their intellectual and ethical development; and that the development of a sense of voice, mind, and self were intricately intertwined."[1] The authors contrast this emphasis on voice with the emphasis on visual metaphors that have been used in mainstream Western culture to depict intellectual and ethical development, equating knowledge with illumination, truth with light.

The physicist Evelyn Fox Keller, who has written extensively about women's approach to science, believes that metaphors of vision reflect traditional Western notions of science in a way that is distinctly male. Keller observes that using visual terms to describe the process of scientific discovery presupposes the scientist's being detached, observing a phenomenon outside himself in a thoroughly objective way.[2] He "steps back" to view reality "with a clear eye," then records truth impassively, "like a camera"; in order to keep vision clear, he runs tests "double blind." Keller contrasts this visually objective view of scientific phenomena with what she finds to be the female scientist's more subjective approach, her understanding of all life as being interconnected, her perception that the knower must always also be part of

222

the known. Keller concludes that vision metaphors are inadequate to describe this more comprehensive female approach; terms that imply interconnectedness are needed.

Carol Gilligan extends her description of the female value for connection far beyond the parameters of science. Like Keller, she argues that males tend to view truth as abstract and objective, while women perceive it as contextual, affected by and emerging from human circumstance. Metaphors based on listening and speaking thus reflect this contextual bias, since what is *heard* always influences what is *said*. Gilligan's concept of "a different voice" both defines female development and encompasses women's value for connectedness.

The authors of *Women's Ways of Knowing* note that, unlike the eye, the ear operates by registering subtle changes. Unlike seeing, which is a one-way process, speaking and listening suggest dialogue and interaction.[3] A vision may exist alone, in the mind of a single human being—it can still be a vision if it remains uncommunicated. But a voice cannot be a voice unless someone is there to hear it; it finds its form in the process of interaction. Thus voice may be defined not just as a vocal instrument, but as a mode of communicating information and, more subtly, sensibility.

We can conclude, then, that women's way of leading emphasizes the role of voice over that of vision. The woman leader's voice is a means both for presenting herself and what she knows about the world, and for eliciting a response. Her vision of her company might define its ends, but her voice is the means for getting that vision across. And it is in this method, in this concern for means along with ends, that the value for connectedness is nurtured.

Each of the women in the diary studies speaks with a distinctive voice. Frances Hesselbein speaks calmly and deliberately, always giving the impression of choosing her words, shaping and managing her tone. Dorothy Brunson suits her voice to the occasion—teasing, reconciling, confronting, needling, questioning, cajoling, spurring to action; always with zest, directness, and a sense of humor. Barbara Grogan's voice is warm, vibrant, and cheerful, with a note of appreciative surprise at the little events of every day. Nancy Badore's voice is passionate and provocative, given to extremes, confident, unafraid of sounding foolish.

Each woman's voice is both a unique expression of her own personality and an instrument for conveying and guiding her vision of how her organization should be run. Frances Hesselbein's deliberativeness, Dorothy Brunson's imaginative directness, Barbara Grogan's gift for organized spontaneity, Nancy Badore's involvement in stimulating change: each woman's management style finds expression in her voice. And by suiting her tone to her words and her words to her tone, each is able both to model her values and find a way to instruct, influence, and persuade others to share those values.

This ability to model and persuade is of particular importance in an organization where authority is not imposed from the top down in hierarchical fashion. In a web structure, where talent is nurtured and encouraged rather than commanded, and a variety of interconnections exist, influence and persuasion take the place of giving orders. The lines of authority are less defined, more dependent upon a moral center. Compassion, empathy, inspiration, and direction—all aspects of nurturance—are connective values, better communicated by voice, by tone, than by vision.

The concern of the women in the diary studies with their written correspondence is natural in this context, for correspondence is a reflection and a record of the voice. Frances Hesselbein's deliberation and care at the Dictaphone, Barbara Grogan's writing her letters in longhand—both reflect their consciousness of the need to maintain the tone they have set in written as well as verbal interactions. Both Frances Hesselbein and Dorothy Brunson expected correspondence with their organizations to be answered within three days, promptness being an aspect of their voices.

As already noted, authority in the structure of the web has a teacherlike quality. And certainly a leader using her voice to model and persuade reflects a teacher's dual way of communicating with her students. A teacher uses her voice all day long in order to "raise up others" and "help them find their voices," as the authors of *Women's Ways of Knowing* observe. Thus implicit in the use of voice as an instrument of leadership is the notion that care and empowerment are leadership tasks.

Each of the women in the diary studies is easy to visualize as a teacher, and each is conscientious about imparting "lessons." On an earlier day that I spent with Frances Hesselbein, she called in a young woman from the Girl Scouts' publicity department before doing a telephone interview with a magazine reporter. The young woman's job was simply to sit and listen to the interview so that she would know how such a task should be done. Frances Hesselbein used her speaker phone; as the young woman listened, she took notes. The meeting was structured as a lesson.

Similarly, Dorothy Brunson's habit of sitting with an employee while he or she cleaned out a desk drawer took the form of a lesson. So did her request that employees wanting a raise write out all their reasons and present them to her. This functioned as an exercise in getting them to think, to reason, to put their financial needs in context by having to back up their argument. She also gave spontaneous little quizzes when she talked to her people. "I'll ask them questions, show them what they need to know."

Nancy Badore, having spent years in academia getting her Ph.D., ran her three-hour roundtable meeting like a Socratic dialogue, pushing her team members to ask more questions, to look a little further. Not to push themselves harder or to work more, but to think more deeply and range more widely in considering implications; the idea was to stimulate their imaginations. And Barbara Grogan, running the Governor's Small Business Advisory Council meeting, had a good teacher's spontaneous gift for fun, laughing as she "called the class to order." Like Nancy Badore, she asked questions that encouraged people to use their imaginations, stopping the discussion at various moments in order to underline specific points: "Here's something we really need to examine. This could be important!" In stressing empowerment and human development rather than subordination to the chain of command, this type of leadership allows scope for what Jean Baker Miller calls the "affiliative focus."[4] She defines this as an overriding value for responsibility and interconnection, rather than the quest for authority and autonomy. Like Carol Gilligan, she finds this focus to be characteristic of women.

Nancy Badore noted that she "loved to talk." The same could be said of all the women in the diary studies. Having found ways to express their values in their speech, all were able to let loose and really enjoy themselves during meetings and presentations, giving their personalities full scope. Dorothy Brunson's lust for friendly verbal combat, and the "flow" that both Barbara Grogan and Frances Hesselbein try to instill in their discussions evidence the ease and naturalness of their voices. Watching the women's zestful approach to the verbal challenges of their days, I was reminded of the

227

feeling of musicians when they catch a groove, in the improvisational sense of finding chords that are spontaneous and original expressions, but also hook up with what the rest of the band is playing. When it all comes together, there's a rightness to it, an ease, a sense of rhythm, and always a sense of fun.

In order to use the voice with this kind of spontaneous and expressive pleasure, one must first find one's voice. Nancy Badore specifically identified "finding her voice" as learning to recognize her own strengths and weaknesses, which made her realize that she had "something special to contribute to the company," unique qualities that, though unexpected and out of the ordinary, could be of special help in her job. In evolving a revolutionary format, and fighting to make it work, she found an outlet that allowed her to exercise and express managerial talents that she hadn't known she possessed. Barbara Grogan found her voice in the exhilarating first years of founding her business, after being forced to take her own measure during the painful time of her divorce. The process of discovering that "I could make things work even after feeling my whole life had been shattered," gave her the confidence she needed to "express my *own* values in the way I manage, not feel I had to follow a man's idea of how it should be done." This need to express one's own values within a management style is an essential element in developing one's true voice.

228

Through her policy of helping younger women at Ford, Nancy Badore has come to believe that "Most women don't realize that they're good at their jobs until about five or ten years after men do." This situation may well be responsible for the slight hesitation and rigidity in female middle-managers' voices noted in *The Managerial Woman*[5]—a tone more supervisory than managerial, as the authors observe. It is not difficult to speculate why women in business might take longer to develop confidence than men do, since, as Betty Harragan points out, the organizations in which they work have for the most part been fashioned entirely "without the ideas, brains, and creative instincts of women." And insofar as finding one's voice requires recognizing that one's talents are appropriate to one's work, it seems natural that it would take women longer to find their voices. The structures in which women work were not devised by them, and so are weighted in ways that do not reflect their values.

Finding one's voice releases a lot of energy. Each of the women in the diary studies commented on this extraordinary feeling of release, this ability to relax while swimming with the flow. Frances Hesselbein attributed her remarkable energy and calm to this freeing of herself: "It's not hard work that wears you out, but the repression of your true personality, and I've found a way of working that does not demand that." Dorothy Brunson said that she did not experience the stress that many other people in her business did because she had learned "to be absolutely true to what I believe. As a result, I'm very direct. I think people use up a lot of their best energies trying to hide things—from themselves, and from other people too." And both Nancy Badore and Barbara Grogan talked of having more time to devote to their work because, as Barbara Grogan put it, "I don't have to waste energy trying to be something I'm not."

This notion of being true to oneself is the very essence of finding one's voice. Voice is a mode for manifesting internal truth. But the emphasis is on the manifestation, the expression, not on the truth in itself, as would be the case if one were speaking of finding a vision. Nor, it should be noted, does anyone speak of *finding* a vision; a vision is something that one has. This notion of a search—which is really a search for self—makes explicit how embedded voice is in the process of personal development. *Leading* with a voice is only possible when one has reached a certain level of development as a person; otherwise, the voice will not ring true.

CHAPTER NINE

Reconciling the Efficient and the Humane

In her classic *Toward a New Psychology of Women*, Jean Baker Miller observes that the female values of responsibility, connection, and inclusion have been devalued in our culture, which tends to celebrate the lone hero, the rugged individual. Psychologists in particular, she notes, have tended to equate a strong awareness of human interdependence with a failure to develop a strong and mature sense of self, and they have seen the desire to serve others as neurotic, something to be "worked through."[1] Yet Miller also observes that in recent years this bias has begun to diminish, as alienation, loneliness, family instability, and resulting problems of drugs and random crime have forced the recognition that a sense of human community is much needed in modern culture. In addition, the environmental consciousness that has developed is making even the most obdurate individualists admit that everyone's actions do impact on everyone else.[2]

As a result, the female view that one strengthens oneself by strengthening others is finding greater acceptance, and female values of inclusion and connection are emerging as valuable leadership qualities. As Miller notes, this kind of leadership is precisely what is needed in order to address the alienation that troubles our public sphere institutions—business, politics, medicine, and the law. Much current literature, philosophy, and social commentary focuses on the lack of human connection in these institutions, a lack which has resulted in widespread concern about this culture's inability to organize the fruits of technology to serve human ends. Miller sees this as "perhaps the central problem of the dominant male culture."[3] It amounts to the exaltation of efficiency at the expense of humane values.

What is needed, then, is leaders who can work against these feelings of alienation that affect our institutions, by bridging the gap between the demands of efficiency and the need to nurture the human spirit. Reconciling these values is particularly important in today's competitive economic landscape, where the intelligence, commitment, and enthusiasm of employees are more crucial to the success of an enterprise than they have been in the past. No longer is there a single "right way" to do things, as there was in the industrial era, when employees had simply to master a set of tasks or a predictable routine and then, making as few errors as possible, stick with that. The nature of the information economy, and the demands of the team approach, require employees who can think, participate, speak up, take initiative, and devise new ideas.

But more than just the nature of work is changing; the

nature of people who work is changing too. Employees today are less likely to put up with a workplace that emphasizes efficiency at the expense of meeting human needs. According to a recent report in *The Wall Street Journal*, people entering the workplace today are more concerned with intangibles such as being happy, working in a good environment, and having opportunities for growth, than any group of people in the past.[4] A survey of college students revealed that salary ranked only sixth in importance among a list of job considerations, well behind intangibles like satisfaction and fulfillment, and that people entering today's labor-short job market are comfortable with the notion of changing companies if they experience even a well-paying job as inhumane or stifling.[5]

Given the changing nature both of work and of people who work, there emerges a need for leaders who can stimulate employees to work with zest and spirit. Such leaders must create an ambiance that reflects human values, and devise organizational structures that encourage and nurture human growth. Creating an ambiance here must be understood in the largest sense as setting a tone that expresses a unified vision of why an organization exists, and devising a style that communicates that vision.

ORGANIZING AMBIANCE

The physical space in which an organization functions gives a good indication of its values, of how well it reconciles being efficient with being humane. The organizational spaces that the women in the diary studies helped create all function as visible manifestations of their particular styles of leadership, and in very different ways give impetus to work being done with creativity and zest.

Dorothy Brunson paid deliberate attention to the physical design of the offices of her flagship station, WEBB. She says, "I collect antiques and paintings at home, but I would never surround myself with such things at the office. I believe a feeling of freshness and light is most appropriate for where people work. I get depressed just walking into most CEOs' offices. I see all that heavy expensive furniture, that dark wood and those thick carpets, and I wonder what the guy is trying to prove. Why is he trying to remove himself, create this private Oz? It's certainly inappropriate for a hands-on manager who wants to be involved. I want the style of my office to show that I'm *not* removed. I want my people to feel as if they're part of what's going on. Having lots of fancy things isolates you by proclaiming your status."

In order to facilitate the kind of constant interchange that she believes fosters spirit and fresh ideas, Dorothy Brunson has organized her suite of offices around a large glass-walled central meeting room. The informal spot works for large meetings, but also serves as a kind of "clearing," a place for people to meet and keep in touch. Brunson's own offices (both of them) have windows that open directly onto this central room, and windows cut into other offices also provide a view. In the entire suite, there are no curtains or shades on the outside windows. "I don't want anything that closes people off—from me, from each other, or from the world. Our business thrives on information, on staying in touch, and that's what I try to recreate in my offices."

The main floor of Nancy Badore's Executive Development Center is also organized around a large central open room, this one circular, around which the offices fan out in a weblike structure. This meeting room, where those taking their training meet with members of the staff for the kind of break time that Nancy Badore believes is so important, serves as the heart of the organization. Food, coffee, and soft drinks are set out on buffet tables in this room, to feed those in training and encourage "hanging out." Both the way the space is organized and the way it's used are reminiscent of the central piazza in an Italian town, which serves the function of knitting the populace together. "We like the place to be noisy and messy so that people will feel at ease, so we drag chairs in, do whatever we need to do," says Nancy Badore. She has also introduced the custom of scattering plates of fruit around the offices, both in order to encourage healthy eating and to provide stations for informal encounters. She believes that encouraging such moments is important because "some of the most meaningful exchanges take place during those unplanned moments, when people in an organization have a chance to really get talking."

This drive to provide a way for others to keep in touch lies at the heart of the women's decisions about how to use their organizational spaces. So does their refusal to emphasize their own status. Both these impulses are manifestations of the strategy of the web, in which authority results from strengthening interconnections and drawing others close. Having this as a source of strength eliminates the need for status accoutrements, the function of which is always to define and reinforce distance. Drawing her authority from interconnections, Barbara Grogan has no need to assert her role as boss by having a separate office with a door that closes, or a lot of external space to set it apart. Instead she uses low room dividers and has no door, so that "my people can holler when they need me."

A similar focus is apparent in the way Frances Hesselbein allocates office space in the Girl Scouts' fourteen-story office building in midtown Manhattan. She decided against bunching management team members—who are the "first ring" in her orbit—together on an upper floor, as is common in so many companies as large as the Girl Scouts. "Our idea was to put management team members with the people they worked with, not to use office allocation to make a statement about who's 'on top'—who's on the highest floor, or closest to the president.

That sort of status location has no importance around here. Management team members have their offices on the same floor as their support staff so they can be in the *middle* of what's going on."

The women's spaces are not only organized in ways that foster and engage the human spirit; they are also efficient means for facilitating interaction and information flow. They contrast with the innate inefficiency of spaces organized to reflect bureaucratic divisions and hierarchical rankings, which not only discourage the spirit, but provide a physical paradigm of limited and rigid channels of access. Such spaces reveal that the exaltation of efficiency at the expense of humane values, which Jean Baker Miller describes as characteristic of our public sphere institutions, is in fact a false dichotomy. A use of space that facilitates interconnection and seeks to encourage communication will be both efficient *and* humane.

But it takes a mind that thinks beyond convention to see that these two principles can be reconciled. A more prosaic and limited definition of efficiency cannot get beyond the assumption of dichotomy. I was particularly struck by the imaginativeness of Nancy Badore's policy of keeping fruit around the office in order both to encourage healthy eating and to provide spontaneous opportunities for interaction. The policy was in total contrast to one that I saw instituted in the company where I was a speechwriter at the very time our unit was charged with trying to persuade employees to take more initiative, be more creative, and think beyond the narrow confines of their job descriptions. In the midst of that campaign, even as we tried to reassure people that they mattered to the company, the head of our division abruptly ordered all the water coolers removed. Not only had he decided that providing fresh healthful water to employees was a waste of corporate profits (although extravagant perks for executives remained in place), he also believed that providing a place on every floor where people could gather spontaneously encouraged employees to fritter away time chatting with one another, rather than remaining at their desks, poring over their work. And yet it was obvious to anyone who moved around the floor that many of people's most imaginative ideas resulted from just such informal talk, from casual discussion of company policy and needs. The removal of the water coolers, a small gesture in itself, came to epitomize the company's values: sacrificing the human spirit in the interests of a narrow vision of efficiency that ended up being inefficient.

But perhaps it takes an outsider's eye to see beneath such surface dichotomies, to understand how water coolers (or bowls of fruit) could be ultimately efficient. And here is a perfect example of how women's position as historic outsiders in the corporation can provide them with an advantage in a time of rapid change. Many of the rituals of corporate life are not only deadening to the spirit, but also inefficient; ways of reinforcing status that have nothing at all to do with how the job gets done.

Rather, they are ways for exemplifying what Alfred Sloan, former president of General Motors, defined as "professionalism"—that kind of autonomy and distance that become self-perpetuating. Rarely are these rituals questioned so long as insiders who share similar and established values dominate positions of leadership.

An example is a story that Marlene Sanders, the former network executive and television reporter, told at a recent media conference in Washington, D.C.[6] Sanders related how, upon being made corporate VP at her network, she was warned that she would have to learn to play one-draw poker, skill at the game being essential among the brass. She studied the game until she mastered it, imagining that it must be important, perhaps providing a useful model of corporate strategy. A few weeks later, while flying with the other New York vice presidents (all male) to Los Angeles, she spent the entire flight relieving the men of their money.

"They were *so* impressed. I had proven I could keep up with the boys who sat at the big table. I had passed their testing ritual, showed I could be as macho as them. But I realized very quickly that that was *the only purpose* the game served—it was a way of proving you were a worthy member of the club. But that worthiness had absolutely *nothing* to do with the execution of your job! Furthermore, the game provided a way to avoid discussing what was really important, preparing for our meeting, or even just getting to know one another. It was a way of distancing, not communicating, and as our plane

landed in L.A. I couldn't help help thinking what a co-
lossal waste of five perfectly good hours it had been.
And one thing I felt sure of: if it had been a group of
women, we would never have wasted our time on such
a childish game!"

The poker game provided a way for the men in the
group to assert their need for status, to create definable
winners and losers. In such competitive tests, a participant communicates by posing rather than by speaking
and listening, which casts relationships into a purely
symbolic realm. Like the isolated CEO's office with in-
timidatingly huge furniture and thick absorbent rugs,
games that serve no purpose except to prove that you
are a "winner" ultimately impede the flow of communication.

LISTENING

Communication is what defines the style of leadership
that reconciles efficiency with human values. Communication involves using the voice as an instrument to disseminate vision, and also stresses the crucial role that
listening plays. But in the hierarchical pyramid, being a
skilled listener is not a function of leadership, since information is filtered on its way up and decisions passed
down.

The women in the diary studies are all skilled listeners; it was a strong aspect of their management style.
They used listening both as a tool to gather information

that had bearing on managerial decisions, and as a way of making the people in their organizations feel that their ideas and beliefs were of value. Frances Hesselbein viewed listening as a discipline that lay at the very heart of her kind of leadership. In her view, a good leader was one who knew "exactly how to bring out what's best in people," and only a leader who really listened could hope to do this. Her policy of making herself personally available to hear whatever suggestions people in her company had to make—along with her refusal to look at her watch whenever anyone was talking—all evidenced her belief in the value of careful and patient listening.

For Dorothy Brunson, listening was the method she used to find the clues she needed in order to know how to handle a person. Listening told her what role she should adopt in a given situation, what aspect of herself she should play up. At Nancy Badore's Executive Development Center, which had as its mission teaching managers to "talk up the ladder," getting leaders to *listen down the ladder* was the implicit corollary. The changes in Ford's management style, in which Nancy Badore has played a part, provide an example of the role of listening in the reinvented corporation. The very crux of the company's managerial revolution has lain in requiring leaders who had previously been exclusively speakers to *listen* to what their people have to say.

Listening is perhaps the prototypical female skill. Studies on gender differences in the use of language suggest that men tend to speak far more than women, while women do more of the listening. Furthermore, the quality of women's listening is different—more intense, more thoughtful, more attentive.[7] The differences between the sexes are large and persistent in this regard, and apply both in the workplace and at home, despite many men's persistent belief that women are the "gabbers" while they are the strong, silent types.[8] But women's greater aptitude for and skill in listening hardly comes as a surprise, since listening is characteristic of subordinates, who survive by reading the emotions, discerning the desires, and anticipating the needs of those in control.

Yet, as the diary studies make clear, this propensity to listen remains with women when they have moved far beyond subordinate positions. Even when they find their voices, and start to speak assertively as leaders, women nevertheless retain a strong value and talent for listening. That this is so implies that listening is not just a consequence of subordinate status, but something women value in itself. And indeed, in *A Different Voice*, Carol Gilligan notes that the deference women exhibit in their ability and willingness to listen "is rooted not just in social subordination, but also *in the substance of their moral concern.*"[9] It is a skill intrinsic to their values for responsibility, interconnection, and inclusion, not simply a result of their position as "the second sex." Women value listening as a way of making others feel comfortable and important, and as a means of encouraging others to find their own voices and grow. Sara Ruddick, in her book *Maternal Thinking*, recognizes listening as an aspect of the "labor of care"[10] that is characteristic of how mothers nurture growth in their children. Thus a propensity and value for listening persists even when women assume leadership positions; it is an essential part of the female talent for "raising others up and drawing them forth." It is both a manifestation of moral concern that reflects women's human values, and an efficient means of stimulating the flow of information.

One of the women I interviewed when preparing to write this book talked about what she called "analytic listening," an essential element of her management style. Nancy Singer is the president and CEO of Premier Banks, a six-bank division of the First of America Corporation, a holding company in the Midwest. With responsibility for 340 employees, she manages to schedule in regular time several early mornings a week so that people can come by her office just to talk.

Nancy Singer believes that most managers make the mistake of assuming that a single style of management works with everyone. "That's all wrong. Different things work with different people, but you can only know what works with who by taking the time to get to know your people. And that does not mean knowing them in broad strokes. You have to know the details, understand the fine strokes of who your people are. And that means listening to what they have to say—about themselves, about their work, about what they want from the future."[11]

As she listens, Singer is constantly analyzing. "I ask myself, what precisely motivates this person? Is it challenge? A desire to enjoy the work? Or is the motivation purely monetary? Does this person need approval from the group? How ambitious is he? What are his aspirations? Is his family and personal life a major consideration, or is his career his primary focus? When I have that kind of information I can decide how to act—who needs stroking, who needs space, who needs more mentoring. Listening helps me know when to promote, when to challenge, when to encourage, when to caution. It helps me guide the fit between a person and his or her job. To manage expectations—that's what's important! But you can't do it unless you gather detailed information, and that means listening with sensitivity to what people say."

Singer describes the process as a synthesis of intellectual power and emotional response. "What it's really all about is bringing my logical analytic skills to bear in the service of human understanding." Thus analytic listening is a skill that bridges the apparent dichotomy between a bottom-line focus and a concern for people, between ends and means, between efficient and humane.

COLLABORATIVE
NEGOTIATION

Dorothy Brunson and Barbara Grogan, when asked what they viewed as their greatest strengths, both said that they were good negotiators. Dorothy Brunson's delight in the process was evident: "Let's negotiate it!" was her immediate response when anyone asked her for something. But negotiating for her was not so much a way of winning as a process that enabled her to build relationships. Her focus was both on getting a deal that served her company's interests and on keeping the other party happy, so that he or she would "keep coming back for more." Thus, by focusing on the long-term interaction, she used negotiation to bridge the gap between the efficient and the humane.

According to Leonard Greenhalgh, a professor at the Amos Tuck School of Business Administration at Dartmouth University, this approach to negotiation as a collaborate effort with long-term implications is characteristic of women. Greenhalgh has done extensive research both on what makes an effective negotiator, and on gender differences in negotiating styles. He has concluded from his studies that women's values for interdependence and mutuality make them treat negotiations within the context of continuing relationships that require contact, interaction, and agreement. By contrast, men's focus on independence, competitiveness, and autonomy makes them more likely to see negotiations as an opportunity for winning or besting an opponent than for collaborating or building a relationship.[12]

Greenhalgh points out that sports metaphors of winning, losing, and scoring points have largely governed notions of negotiations in the public realm as they have been presided over by men. He attributes this to the role that sports play in male development, and to the prevalence of competitive games among male children, which he contrasts with the relationship-oriented games played by girls. He notes that girls' games teach them the importance of preserving and enhancing relationships—a long-term focus—while boys' games teach them to preserve and enhance their own feelings of self-worth at the expense of relationships—a competitive focus that is of necessity short-term.[13] Thus Greenhalgh, in contrast to observers like Betty Harragan and the authors of *The Managerial Woman,* does not view girls' games as a pointless waste of time, but as valuable training for the task of fostering human relationships.

In addition, he cites a debilitating tendency among men to rely on rules to enforce agreements, in accord with the sports metaphor of "playing by the rules." This emphasis encourages a legalistic frame of mind that, by undermining and devaluing the importance of trust, increases a negotiator's tendency to litigate disputes. Also, Greenhalgh notes that sports norms do not permit players to let one team win this week in exchange for reciprocal leniency by the other team next week, since "the history and future of the ongoing relationship between contestants is irrelevant in sports."[14]

Because of women's gift for collaborative agreement and their concern with fostering relationships in the long term, Greenhalgh would like to see women leaders play a more active role in negotiating, for example, international treaties. He views many problems on the world stage, as well as in American business, as resulting from men's tendency to focus on winning and their eagerness to resort to legalistic resolutions.

As women's leadership qualities come to play a more dominant role in the public sphere, their particular aptitudes for long-term negotiating, analytic listening, and creating an ambiance in which people work with zest and spirit will help reconcile the split between the ideals of being efficient and being humane. This integration of female values is already producing a more collaborative kind of leadership, and changing the very ideal of what strong leadership actually is. The old lone hero leader is increasingly being recognized as not only deadening to the human spirit, but also ultimately inefficient. The Ford Motor Company, seeking a phrase to express the essence of its managerial revolution, adopted a motto that expresses this recognition: *"No more heroes!"* Thus as the values, skills, and experience of women, so long restricted to the private, domestic sphere, are integrated into the public realm, what Jean Baker Miller calls women's "much greater sense of the pleasure of close connection with physical, emotional, and mental growth than men"[15] will create an environment that meets the needs of people who work today.

CHAPTER TEN

The End of the Warrior Age

Every one of our public fields of endeavor—business, government, medicine, law, technology, urban design—has been shaped by the ideals, images, values, and language of the Warrior. The Warrior is the traditional male hero who charges into the battle with the aim of dominating and winning, and in the process defines and strengthens himself. His quest is not only for dominance, but also for autonomy, which, as Carol Gilligan points out, is the prime task of male development.[1] Thus needs for autonomy, competition, and control have been built into the very structure of those organizations that have served our culture in the public realm.

So long as Warrior values dominated the public realm, the role of women has been, in Jean Baker Miller's phrase, to serve as "carriers" for all those qualities deemed too soft for the demands of battle.[2] Nurturing, mercy, participating in the growth of others, fostering human connection—these were all qualities that the Warrior could not afford to indulge or explore, lest they weaken his resolve to compete. Thus the private, domestic sphere over which women reigned became the repository of humane and caring values, while the world of work and politics flourished by ruthless competition. The Warrior's wife created an oasis to which he could repair for physical and spiritual refreshment before returning to the rigors of the fray. Assigned to different sexes and different realms, these dualistic divisions deprived each sex and realm of the full range of human possibility. Each was left impoverished, stunted, only half complete.

Splitting off values for human connection and interdependence and assigning them to the female sphere has left the public world a hostile place, in thrall to notions of competition that have become more dangerous as technology has become more potent. Our culture's "inability to harness technology to serve human ends," noted by Jean Baker Miller, has resulted in the strain of having to live with the threat of nuclear apocalypse on one hand, and the reality of environmental degradation on the other. The old Warrior virtues—fearlessness, a thirst for combat, single-minded devotion to an ideal, aggression, the ability to conceptualize the other as the enemy, the fierce need to prove oneself in contests—all these once served the evolutionary human purpose of mobilizing the strongest adult males to preserve and protect other members of the immediate tribe. But advanced technology has turned those virtues into liabilities; aggressive heroics now threaten the survival of the larger tribe, the human race.

The psychologist Carol Pearson, writing in *The Hero*

Within, notes that the inadequacy of the Warrior system has long been a subject of modern literature, the primary theme of which is alienation and despair.[3] For more than seventy-five years, the image of "the Waste Land" has predominated in literature as a way of expressing the twentieth-century human condition. Since the Second World War, popular and scholarly studies about feelings of pointlessness, sterility, and the separation from nature in modern life have continued to capture the public imagination. The antihero has replaced the hero as the central figure in our literature precisely because the hero myth has come to seem outmoded in a world that too well knows the human cost of pure Warrior values.

The integration of the feminine principles into the public realm offers hope for healing this condition, returning a concern for the nurturing and fostering of life to our public sphere, and decreasing the emphasis on competition—whether to build the highest building, or to "win" a totally abstract arms race. Thus women's entry into the public sphere can be seen not merely as the result of contemporary economic pressures, the high rate of divorce, or the success of the feminist movement, but rather as a profound evolutionary response to a pervasive cultural crisis. Feminine principles are entering the public realm because *we can no longer afford* to restrict them to the private domestic sphere, nor allow a public culture obsessed with Warrior values to control human destiny if we are to survive.

255

Drawing on Jung's study of symbols, Carol Pearson points out that under the old dichotomized system, the female heroic archetype was the Martyr. The Martyr's central tasks are care, sacrifice, and redemptive suffering; the Martyr's central recognition is, "I am not the only person in this world." This puts the Martyr in total contrast to the Warrior, whose central tasks are individuation, achievement, and action, and whose chief recognition is of his own importance and ability to make a difference in the world. Pearson does not reject the validity or worth of either archetype, but instead proposes that our culture move beyond them to acknowledge a new kind of hero that unites the qualities of both: the Magician.[4]

The Magician incorporates the Martyr's emphasis on care and serving others with the Warrior's ability to affect his environment by the exercise of discipline, struggle, and will. Thus the Magician knows how to sacrifice and give care without losing personal identity, and how to work hard to achieve something without getting caught up in an unceasing competitive struggle. At the Magician's level, Pearson writes, dualities begin to break down. Magicians see beyond apparent dichotomies of male and female, ends and means, efficiency and humanity, mastery and nurturance, logic and intuition. Instead, they focus on the interconnections that bind all human beings and relate events to one another; they take the long view because they see the relation of the present to the future.[5]

It is this awareness of interconnections that enables Magicians, in Pearson's words, "to move with the energy of the universe and to attract what is needed by laws of synchronicity, so that the ease of the Magician's inter-action with the universe seems like magic."[6] "Synchron-icity" is a Jungian concept that means "meaningful coincidences" or acausal connections—as when you go into a bookstore and the very book you need but did not even know existed falls into your hands. This interaction is similar to what Joseph Campbell describes as occur-ring when an individual finds his or her true path: the sensation of being helped by "hidden hands," of finding doors that open, the feeling that "you have put yourself on a kind of track that has been there all the while, waiting for you; and the life that you ought to be living is the one that you are living."[7] This finding of one's path is similar to the finding of one's voice noted by the women in the diary studies—realizing that one's own talents and experiences make one uniquely suited to the task that one has chosen to do in life.

Pearson notes that Magicians in all cultures are asso-ciated with circles. They draw magic circles and put themselves in the middle, structuring the world around them as a web. From inside, they "act as magnets who attract and galvanize positive energy for change by iden-tifying places where growth can occur for individuals, institutions, or social groups, and then by fostering that growth."[8] Taking opportunities as they come, they build up power by empowering others, valuing connections instead of competition. They recognize that, in Barbara Grogan's words, "All ships rise when the tide rises," so they use their power to effect a rising of the tide.

Pearson sees Magicians as characterized above all by receptiveness: "The Magician's great talent is for tapping into and drawing strength from energy sources outside herself." This is Dorothy Brunson's way of working, likening herself to a transmitter, "picking up signals from everywhere, and then beaming them out to wherever they need to go." And certainly the women in the diary studies, with their profound values for interconnection and responsibility, their ecological view, their focus on the long term, and their talent for building up strength by building up others, provide examples of the Magician's way. Each has mastered the Warrior skills of discipline, will, and struggle necessary to achieve success in the public realm, but then moved beyond them to provide models of what leadership can become when guided by the feminine principles.

N O T E S

INTRODUCTION

1. Harragan, Betty Lehan. *Games Mother Never Taught You.* New York: Warner Books, 1977, pp. 42–45.
2. Ibid., pp. 79–89.
3. Ibid., p. 72; p. 43.
4. Hennig, Margaret, and Jardim, Anne. *The Managerial Woman.* New York: Pocket Books, 1976, p. 39.
5. Ibid., p. 33.
6. Ibid., p. 51.
7. Harragan, p. 45.
8. Ibid., p. 58.
9. The Conference Board. *Women in the Corporation: The Value Added.* May 1988. Section One, Facts on Working Women. Data from government sources, pp. 13–27.
10. Naisbitt, John, and Aburdene, Patricia. *Reinventing the Corporation.* New York: Warner Books, 1986, p. 51.
11. Ibid., p. 242.

CHAPTER ONE

1. Conversation with the author, March 17, 1989.
2. Mintzberg, Henry. *The Nature of Managerial Work.* New York: Harper & Row, 1973, pp. vii–x.
3. Conversation with the author, August 31, 1989.
4. Mintzberg, pp. 29–30.
5. Hennig and Jardim, p. 39.
6. Halper, Jan. *Quiet Desperation: The Truth About Successful Men.* New York: Warner Books, 1988, pp. 30–35.
7. *Time* magazine, July 4, 1988., p. 54. Source: Small Business Administration.
8. Gilligan, Carol. *In a Different Voice.* Cambridge: Harvard University Press, 1982.
9. Miller, Jean Baker. *Toward a New Psychology of Women.* Boston: Beacon Press, 1976.
10. Hennig and Jardim, p. 53.
11. The Conference Board, pp. 13–27.
12. Harragan, p. 39.
13. This according to CVR associate Deborah Hefflich, who compiled research from the results of training sessions with 1,926 managers.
14. The Conference Board, pp. 7–29.
15. Mintzberg, Appendix C, pp. 230–77.
16. Halper, pp. 33–37.
17. Campbell, Joseph, with Moyers, Bill. *The Power of Myth.* New York: Doubleday, 1988, pp. 117–21.
18. Quoted, Women and Men in the Media Conference, The National Press Club, Washington, D.C., April 10, 1989.

19. Quoted Lipsyte, Robert. *SportsWorld*. New York: Quadrangle Books, 1975, p. 51.
20. Naisbitt and Aburdene, p. 72.
21. For example: Harragan and Hennig and Jardim. See also Gilligan's rebuttal of prejudices against girls' games, specifically Janet Lever's studies.
22. Gilligan, pp. 11–14.
23. Ibid., pp. 14–22.
24. Harragan, p. 39.
25. Naisbitt and Aburdene, p. 242.

CHAPTER TWO

1. Gilligan, p. 62.
2. Ibid., p. 61ff.
3. Naisbitt and Aburdene, P. 43–44.
4. Ibid., p. 57–59.
5. Hennig and Jardim, p. 33.
6. Interview in *Mirabella*, September 1989.
7. White, E.B., *Charlotte's Web*. New York: Harper & Row, 1952, p. 67.

CHAPTER FOUR

1. Interview in *Across the Board*, published by The Conference Board. March 1989.

CHAPTER SIX

1. Doody, Alton, F., and Bingaman, Ron. *Reinventing the Wheels: Ford's Spectacular Comeback.* Cambridge: Ballinger, 1988, pp. 40–45.

CHAPTER EIGHT

1. Belenky, Mary Field; Clinchy, Blythe McVicker; Goldberger, Nancy Rule; Tarule, Jill Mattuck. *Women's Ways of Knowing.* New York: Basic Books, 1989, p. 18.
2. Quoted, ibid., pp. 18–20.
3. Ibid., pp. 18-20.
4. Miller, p. 85ff.
5. Hennig and Jardim, pp. 58-61.

CHAPTER NINE

1. Miller, pp. 24–25.
2. Ibid., pp. 40–47.
3. Ibid., p. 24.
4. *The Wall Street Journal,* October 26, 1988, p. 1.
5. Ibid., p. 1.
6. Quoted at Women and Men in Media Conference.
7. Belenky, Clinchy, et al., pp. 44–45.
8. Ibid., p. 45.
9. Gilligan, p. 16.
10. Ruddick, Sara. *Maternal Thinking: Toward a Politics of Peace.* Boston: Beacon Press, 1989, pp. 82–102.

11. Interview with the author, April 27, 1989.
12. Greenhalgh, Leonard. "Effects of Sex-Role Differences on Approach to Interpersonal and Interorganizational Negotiations." Private paper, 1985.
13. Greenhalgh, Leonard. "The Case Against Winning in Negotiations," *Negotiation Journal*, April 1987, pp. 167–73.
14. Ibid., p. 171.
15. Miller, p. 40.

CHAPTER TEN

1. Gilligan, p. 8.
2. Miller, p. 86.
3. Pearson, Carol. *The Hero Within: Six Archetypes We Live By*. San Francisco: Harper & Row, 1986, pp. 1–3.
4. Ibid., pp. 116–18.
5. Ibid., p. 6.
6. Ibid., p. 5.
7. Campbell, p. 120.
8. Pearson, p. 119.

HERE'S A SNEAK PREVIEW OF
SALLY HELGESEN'S LATEST CURRENCY BOOK,
THE WEB OF INCLUSION,
NOW AVAILABLE WHEREVER BOOKS ARE SOLD.

EXCERPT:

THE WEB
OF INCLUSION
by Sally Helgesen

The women I studied [in *The Female Advantage*] were
vividly different, and ran organizations that were
wildly diverse . . . Nevertheless, I noticed many
similarities in their style of leading, their presumptions about what motivates people, their goals,
and the ways in which they accomplished their
tasks . . .

In the process of devising ways of leading that
made sense to *them*, the women I studied had built
profoundly integrated and organic organizations,
in which the focus was on nurturing good relationships; in which the niceties of hierarchical rank and
distinction played little part; and in which lines of

265

communication were multiple, open, and diffuse. I noted that the women tended to put themselves at the center of their organizations rather than at the top, thus emphasizing both accessibility and equality, and that they labored constantly to include people in their decision-making. This had the effect of undermining the boundaries so characteristic of mainstream organizations, with their strict job descriptions, categorization of people according to rank, and restrictions on the flow of information.

In some cases, the structures devised by the women were explicit, codified in organizational charts that were deliberately circular as opposed to being top-down. But more often, the structures were discernible mainly in the daily rhythms of how the businesses were run—how time was used, what titles people assumed, how physical space was allotted, the means by which people talked to one another and reached decisions. There was no recognized name or category for what the women were doing, but because I needed a way to describe their organizations, I began referring to them as "webs of inclusion."

The notion stirred a lot of interest. People from around the country wrote me to describe how they too were using a web-like approach to doing their work and structuring the organizations of which they were a part . . . "I thought it was just *my* style, but now I find it's *a* style" was a frequent comment. I heard from many women, of course— entrepreneurs, executives, teachers, nurses, nuns. But I also heard from men—a lawyer for a high-tech firm, an executive who had left General Motors, the head of a big-city hospital, a black sales executive who felt his experience was mirrored in my book.

I also had a response from the military—a number of naval officers, and a general who taught leadership at the U.S. Army War College. All were fascinated by alternatives to traditional top-down structures—of which the military is of course the very model and prototype—and intrigued by the role women might play in helping to devise something else. They also wanted me to know that men who had broken away from traditional hierarchical ways of thinking and leading had an enormous contribution to make in what they believed was the inevitable transformation of our major institutions.

The response surprised me. It was fairly easy to see why the women in the diary studies had structured their companies in innovative ways, for they came as outsiders to positions of leadership in the public sphere. Indeed, it is not too extreme to say that all of our major public sphere organizations have been built, structured, reformed, and refined virtually without the input or ideas of women. Thus it only makes sense that women, coming now to assume public leadership for the first time to any degree, would cast a fresh and critical eye at how our organizations are structured and led.

But many men today also perceive themselves as outsiders to mainstream organizations, as my male correspondents were eager to point out. Over the last decade especially, men have begun to feel increasingly alienated from and critical of the top-down hierarchies that have long set the pattern for how we organize our public world. The reasons are many. The demise of the old "Organization Man" era institutions, which promised lifetime security in exchange for loyalty and the dutiful assumption of a predefined role, has meant that men today do not necessarily look upon the organizations that employ them with the unquestioning perspective of the insider. In addition, as the former GM executive who wrote me noted, many men have grown disillusioned with traditional chain-of-command leadership through watching their own companies flounder because of bad decisions made by insulated executives handing down directives from the top. Then too, the blurring of lines between what were formerly men's and women's exclusive domains has made some men more open to learning things from women.

Thus, while it is surely no accident that "the web of inclusion" should have been identified in a study of women's organizations, the structure has a significance and utility that far transcend the bounds of gender. This is particularly true now, when all of our institutions—business, medical, legal, educational, governmental, and religious—are engaged in a search for ways to adapt to a transformed environment. As the new century approaches, organizations of every variety are being challenged to reconfigure in ways that will make them better able to take advantage of innovative technologies and more responsive to a vastly expanded market— *while in the process becoming more satisfactory places for people to work.*

This last imperative is no longer simply a question of being moral or decent, but also of making wise use of a valuable resource. In the knowledge-based economy that Peter Drucker foresees as our future, the real value of an organization will lie in its people's ability to think, to process information, to evolve creative solutions to complex problems.

And people simply cannot *think* creatively and well if they do not feel valued, if they do not feel a sense of ownership of their work, if they do not have the freedom to give full scope to their talents. Because the new economy must rely upon well-trained people with high morale, it also demands that organizations move beyond the old Industrial Era mentality that perceived a dichotomy between what is efficient and what is humane.

As Margaret Wheatley observes in *Leadership and the New Science,* we are presently engaged in "nothing less than the search for *new sources of order in our world.*" The architecture of the web of inclusion offers us such a source. The notion of architecture is key here, for the science and art of architecture lie in skillfully relating individual parts to a greater whole, creating a form uniquely appropriate for the exercise of a specific set of functions. The old organizational architecture, with its implicit presumptions of an underlying hierarchical order, its emphasis on rank, boundary, and division, has outlived its usefulness as a metaphor by which we relate individuals to the institutions that employ their labor and shape their lives.

In architectural terms, the most obvious characteristics of the web are that it builds from the center out, and that this building is a never-ending process. The architect of the web works as the spider does, by ceaselessly spinning new tendrils of connection, while also continually strengthening those that already exist. The architect's tools are not force, not the ability to issue commands, but rather providing access and engaging in constant dialogue. Such an architect recognizes that the periphery and the center are interdependent, parts of a fabric, no seam of which can be rent without tearing the whole. Balance and harmony are essential if the periphery is to hold; if only the center is strong, the edges will quickly fray. Thus the leader in a web-like structure must manifest strength by yielding, and secure his or her position by continually augmenting the influence of others.

Because tasks done at the periphery truly matter in the web, those who perform them share directly in the responsibilities and rewards of major undertakings. They thus have far more incentive for full-hearted participation than people in the ranks of traditional top-down organizations, which tend relentlessly to emphasize the importance of those at the top. This aggrandizement of purely positional power leads many organizations to fall prey to a heroes-and-drones syndrome, which deprives those who have not achieved top rank of both autonomy and support. The attitude is reflected in such popular slogans as "Lead, follow, or get out of the way" and, even less appealing, "Unless you're the lead horse, the view never changes." No organization today can hope to thrive with this demoralizing vision of the options available to the majority of its people—a vision that wastes talent and resources, breeds frustration and cynicism, and fosters an atmosphere of us-against-them.

CURRENCY

DOUBLEDAY

Since 1989, Currency Doubleday
has published books on business by
Scientists, Scholars, Artists,
Philosophers, Theologians,
Storytellers, and Practitioners who
challenge readers to make a
difference, not just a living.

CURRENCY DOUBLEDAY BOOKS

The Art of Worldly Wisdom: A Pocket Oracle by Baltasar Gracián, translated by Christopher Maurer

Follow the timeless advice of seventeenth-century Jesuit scholar Baltasar Gracián. Each of the elegantly crafted maxims in this *New York Times* bestseller offers valuable insight on the art of living and the practice of achieving.

0-385-42131-1 / U.S. $17.50 / CAN. $22.50 / Hardcover / 182 pages
Also available on audio tape: 0-553-47115-5 / U.S. $9.99 / CAN. $12.00 / 60 minutes

Control Your Destiny or Someone Else Will: How Jack Welch Is Making General Electric the World's Most Competitive Company by Noel M. Tichy and Stratford Sherman

"Thinking of starting a revolution at your company? Before you do, read Noel M. Tichy and Stratford Sherman's book." —*The Wall Street Journal*

Includes a handbook for revolutionaries.

0-385-24883-0 / U.S. $27.00 / CAN. $35.00 / Hardcover / 384 pages

The Fifth Discipline: The Art and Practice of the Learning Organization by Peter M. Senge

This pathbreaking book on building "learning organizations" provides the tools and methods for freeing organizations of their "learning disabilities." A bestseller since 1990, this book has become the organizational bible at AT&T, Ford, Procter & Gamble, and Apple.

0-385-26094-6 / U.S. $30.00 / CAN. $39.00 / Hardcover / 424 pages
Also available as a Currency paperback: 0-385-26095-4 / U.S. $18.50 / CAN. $25.95
Also available on audio tape: 0-553-47321-2 / U.S. $22.00 / CAN. $27.00 / 240 minutes

The Fifth Discipline Fieldbook: Strategies and Tools for Building a Learning Organization by Peter M. Senge, Art Kleiner, Charlotte Roberts, Rick Ross, and Bryan Smith

This is a participative book of tools and techniques based on Peter M. Senge's bestselling *The Fifth Discipline*. It is a workbook with exercises for both individuals and teams, a sourcebook for approaches and ideas, and a wisdom book of stories told by and about the people who are successfully putting the five disciplines into practice.

0-385-47256-0 / U.S. $29.95 / CAN. $38.95 / Paperback / 576 pages

The Great Game of Business by Jack Stack with Bo Burlingham

This is Jack Stack's primer for open-book management, a management method based on the concept of democracy, the spirit of sports, and the reality of numbers.

0-385-42230-X / U.S. $25.00 / CAN. $30.00 / Hardcover / 256 pages
Also available as a Currency paperback: 0-385-47525-X / U.S. $15.00 / CAN. $21.00
Also available on audio tape: 0-553-47350-6 / U.S. $16.99 / CAN. $23.99 / 180 minutes

The Heart Aroused: Poetry and the Preservation of the Soul in Corporate America by David Whyte

The Heart Aroused proposes a new way to transform the practical need to work into an opportunity for spiritual nourishment. It uses the texts of classic poetry to unlock the secrets of how to live a full life at work.

0-385-42350-0 / U.S. $22.50 / CAN. $29.95 / Hardcover / 320 pages

Leadership Is an Art by Max De Pree

This wise, gemlike book offers a new understanding of leadership. In his national bestseller, Max De Pree said, "Leadership isn't a science or discipline. It is an art; as such it must be felt, experienced, created."

0-385-26496-8 / U.S. $21.00 / CAN. $26.00 / Hardcover / 136 pages

Leadership Jazz by Max De Pree

In this bold and innovative work, the bestselling author of *Leadership Is an Art* draws a compelling and illuminating parallel between leadership and jazz—in which improvisation and rules, inspiration and restraint, must be precisely blended.

0-385-42018-8 / U.S. $20.00 / CAN. $25.00 / Hardcover / 228 pages
Also available on audio tape: 0-553-47080-9 / U.S. $15.99 / CAN. $18.99 / 180 minutes

Money and the Meaning of Life by Jacob Needleman

Readers of this book become philosopher Jacob Needleman's students, puzzling out the emotional grip money has on them.

0-385-26241-8 / U.S. $21.00 / CAN. $26.00 / Hardcover / 336 pages
Also available as a Currency paperback: 0-385-26242-6 / U.S. $15.00 / CAN. $21.00
Also available on audio tape: 0-553-47351-4 / U.S. $16.99 / CAN. $23.99 / 180 minutes

The One to One Future: Building Relationships One Customer at a Time by Don Peppers and Martha Rogers

Peppers's and Rogers's revolutionary "one to one" techniques reveal how to use the affordable technology of the modern era to identify your most loyal customers and create the products they most desire.

0-385-42528-7 / U.S. $22.95 / CAN. $28.95 / Hardcover / 464 pages

The Power of Followership by Robert Kelley

Business has spent billions studying and training leaders while entirely ignoring the rest of the workforce—the followers who actually get the job done. This book turns much-needed attention to what makes an exemplary follower.

0-385-41306-8 / U.S. $22.50 / CAN. $28.00 / Hardcover / 260 pages

The Real Heroes of Business and Not a CEO Among Them by Bill Fromm and Len Schlesinger

The authors reveal the stories, secrets, and strategies of fourteen outstanding service workers, identified through a nationwide search, who deserve to be called real heroes—the true experts in service.

0-385-42555-4 / U.S. $22.50 / CAN. $29.95 / Hardcover / 352 pages

The Republic of Tea: The Story of the Creation of a Business as Told Through the Personal Letters of Its Founders by Mel Ziegler, Patricia Ziegler, and Bill Rosenzweig

The Republic of Tea chronicles the feelings and emotions of three partners as they confront their fears and dreams to create an enormously successful start-up company.

0-385-42056-0 / U.S. $22.50 / CAN. $28.00 / Hardcover / 316 pages
Also available as a Currency paperback: 0-385-42057-9 / U.S. $15.00 / CAN. $21.00

You Are the Message by Roger Ailes with Jon Kraushar

Ailes, media adviser to U. S. presidents, top executives, and celebrities, tells you how to hold an audience in the palm of your hand, how to break through fear, and how to rid yourself of other performance blocks.

0-385-26542-5 / U.S. $12.95 / CAN. $16.95 / Paperback / 224 pages

CURRENCY DOUBLEDAY BOOKS

AVAILABLE AT YOUR LOCAL BOOKSTORE. OR YOU MAY USE THIS COUPON TO ORDER DIRECT.

ISBN	TITLE AND AUTHOR	PRICE	QTY.	TOTAL
42131-1	**The Art of Worldly Wisdom** by Baltasar Gracián, translated by Christopher Maurer	U.S. $17.50 / CAN. $22.50 x	__ =	_____
47115-5	*Also available on audio tape*	U.S. $ 9.99 / CAN. $12.00 x	__ =	_____
24883-0	**Control Your Destiny or Someone Else Will** by Noel M. Tichy and Stratford Sherman	U.S. $27.00 / CAN. $35.00 x	__ =	_____
26094-6	**The Fifth Discipline** by Peter M. Senge	U.S. $30.00 / CAN. $39.00 x	__ =	_____
26095-4	*Also available as a Currency paperback*	U.S. $18.50 / CAN. $25.95 x	__ =	_____
47321-2	*Also available on audio tape*	U.S. $22.00 / CAN. $27.00 x	__ =	_____
47256-0	**The Fifth Discipline Fieldbook** by Peter M. Senge, Art Kleiner, Charlotte Roberts, Rick Ross, and Bryan Smith	U.S. $29.95 / CAN. $38.95 x	__ =	_____
42230-x	**The Great Game of Business** by Jack Stack with Bo Burlingham	U.S. $25.00 / CAN. $30.00 x	__ =	_____
47525-x	*Also available as a Currency paperback*	U.S. $15.00 / CAN. $21.00 x	__ =	_____
47350-6	*Also available on audio tape*	U.S. $16.99 / CAN. $23.99 x	__ =	_____
42350-0	**The Heart Aroused** by David Whyte	U.S. $22.50 / CAN. $29.95 x	__ =	_____
26496-8	**Leadership Is an Art** by Max De Pree	U.S. $21.00 / CAN. $26.00 x	__ =	_____
42018-8	**Leadership Jazz** by Max De Pree	U.S. $20.00 / CAN. $25.00 x	__ =	_____
47080-9	*Also available on audio tape*	U.S. $15.99 / CAN. $18.99 x	__ =	_____
26241-8	**Money and the Meaning of Life** by Jacob Needleman	U.S. $21.00 / CAN. $26.00 x	__ =	_____
26242-6	*Also available as a Currency paperback*	U.S. $15.00 / CAN. $21.00 x	__ =	_____
47351-4	*Also available on audio tape*	U.S. $16.99 / CAN. $23.99 x	__ =	_____
42528-7	**The One to One Future** by Don Peppers and Martha Rogers	U.S. $22.95 / CAN. $28.95 x	__ =	_____
41306-8	**The Power of Followership** by Robert Kelley	U.S. $22.50 / CAN. $28.00 x	__ =	_____
42555-4	**The Real Heroes of Business and Not a CEO Among Them** by Bill Fromm and Len Schlesinger	U.S. $22.50 / CAN. $29.95 x	__ =	_____
42056-0	**The Republic of Tea** by Mel Ziegler, Patricia Ziegler, and Bill Rosenzweig	U.S. $22.50 / CAN. $28.00 x	__ =	_____
42057-9	*Also available as a Currency paperback*	U.S. $15.00 / CAN. $21.00 x	__ =	_____
26542-5	**You Are the Message** by Roger Ailes with Jon Kraushar	U.S. $12.95 / CAN. $16.95 x	__ =	_____

Parcel Post shipping and handling. . . . .(add $2.50 per order; allow 4–6 weeks for delivery)_____
UPS shipping and handling . . . .(add $4.50 per order; allow 2–3 weeks for delivery)_____

TOTAL:_____

Please send me the titles I have indicated above. I am enclosing $_____
Send check or money order (no CODs or cash, please) payable to Doubleday Consumer Services. Prices and availability are subject to change without notice.

Name:_____

Address:_____ Apt. #: _____

City:_____ State:_____ Zip:_____

Send completed coupon and payment to:
Doubleday Consumer Services
Dept. DR 9
2451 South Wolf Road
Des Plaines, IL 60018

DR9–5/95

CURRENCY
DOUBLEDAY